BEETLE BAILEY

NOT REVERSE

by Mort Walker

A TOM DOHERTY ASSOCIATES BOOK

TOR

**PINNACLE BOOKS
NEW YORK**

ISBN : 0 - 523 - 49001 - 1

A Tom Doherty Associates Original

Printed in the United States of America

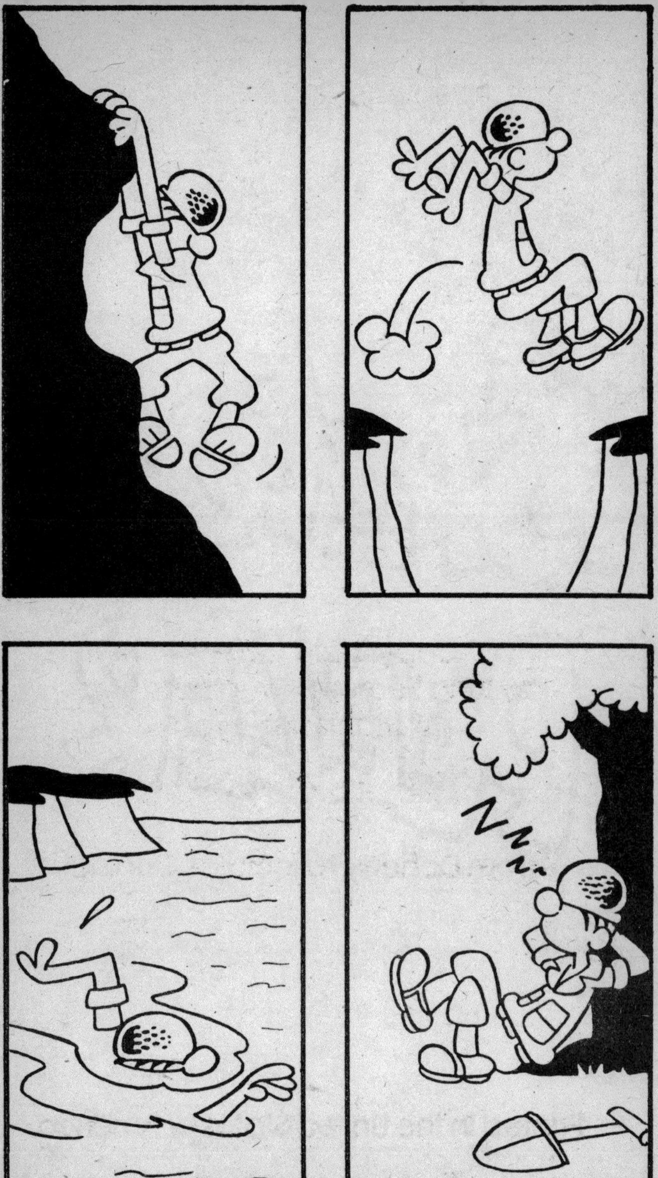

SPEEDY PEELER

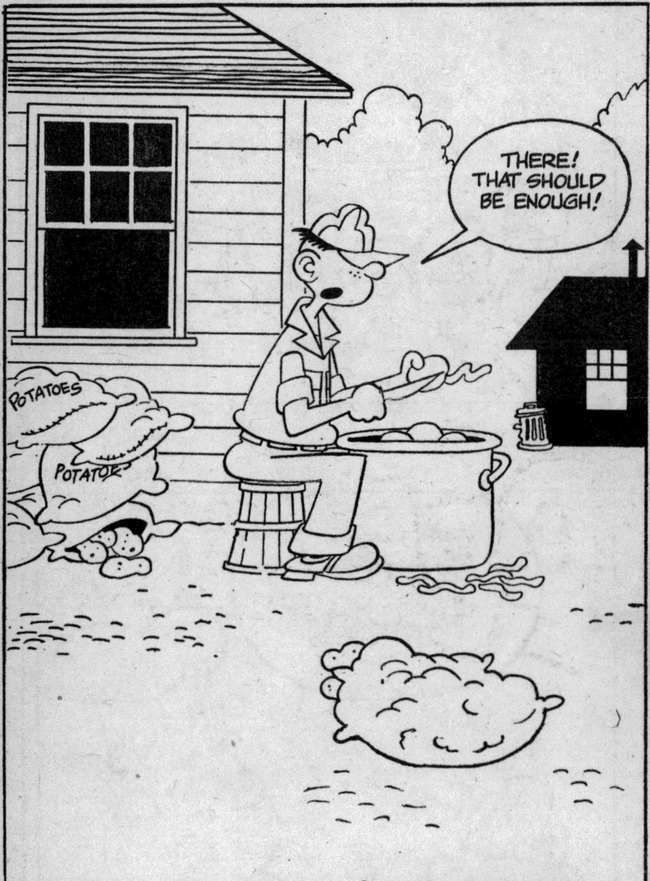
POTATOES
POTATOES
THERE! THAT SHOULD BE ENOUGH!

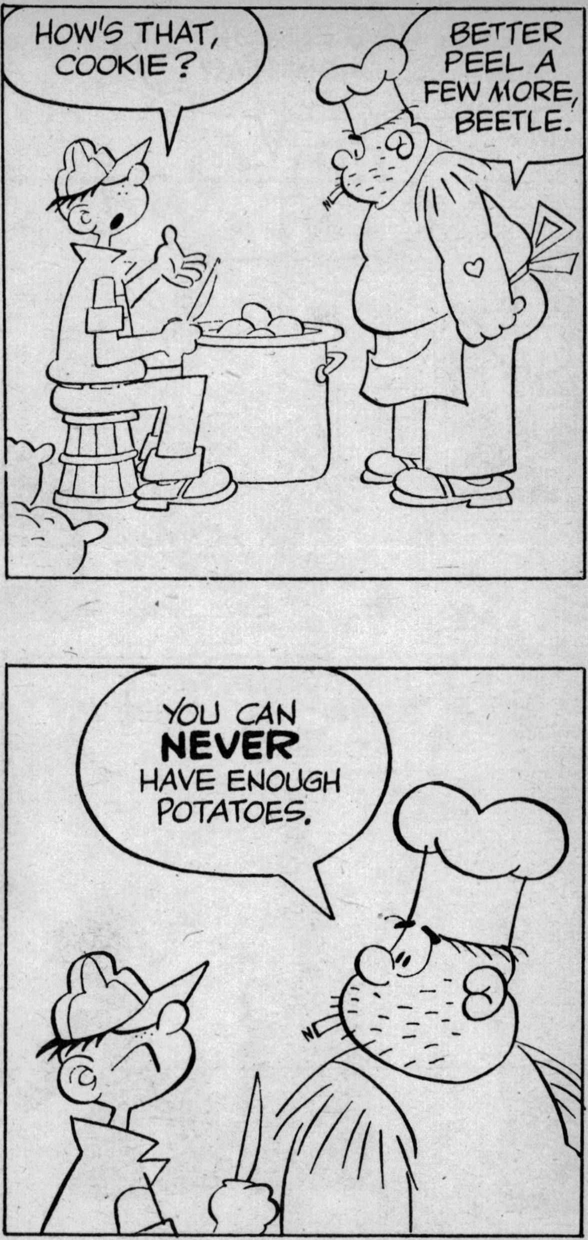
HOW'S THAT, COOKIE?
BETTER PEEL A FEW MORE, BEETLE.
YOU CAN **NEVER** HAVE ENOUGH POTATOES.

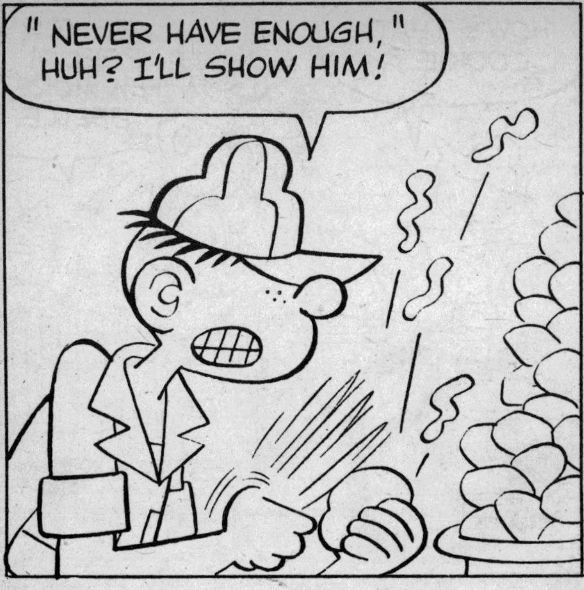
" NEVER HAVE ENOUGH, " HUH? I'LL SHOW HIM!

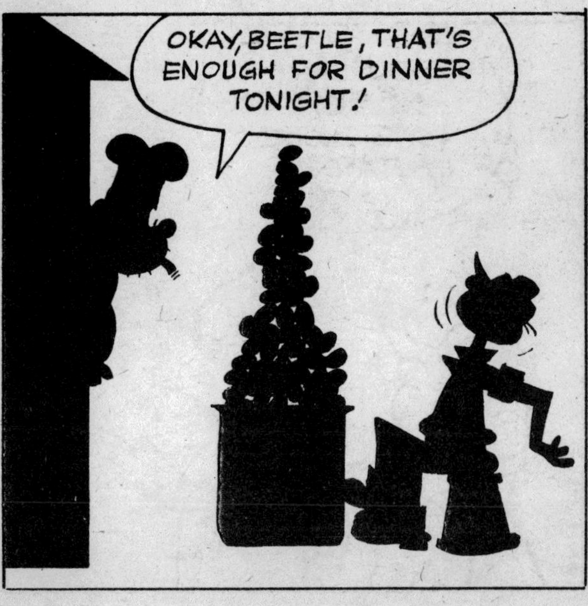
OKAY, BEETLE, THAT'S ENOUGH FOR DINNER TONIGHT!

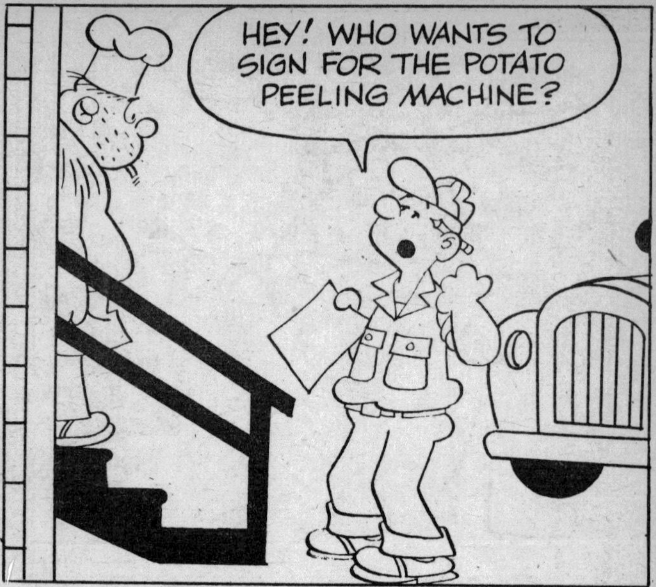
HEY! WHO WANTS TO SIGN FOR THE POTATO PEELING MACHINE?

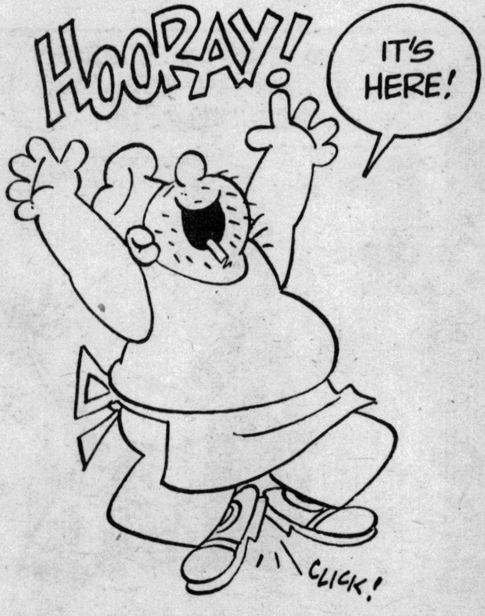
HOORAY!
IT'S HERE!
CLICK!

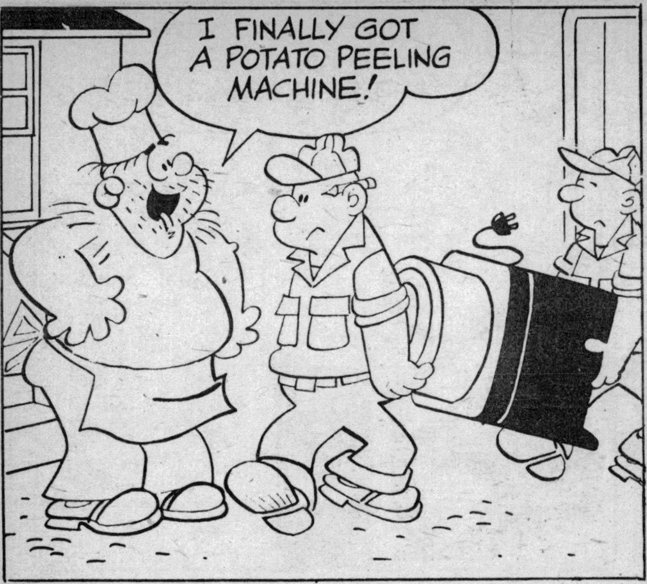
I FINALLY GOT A POTATO PEELING MACHINE!

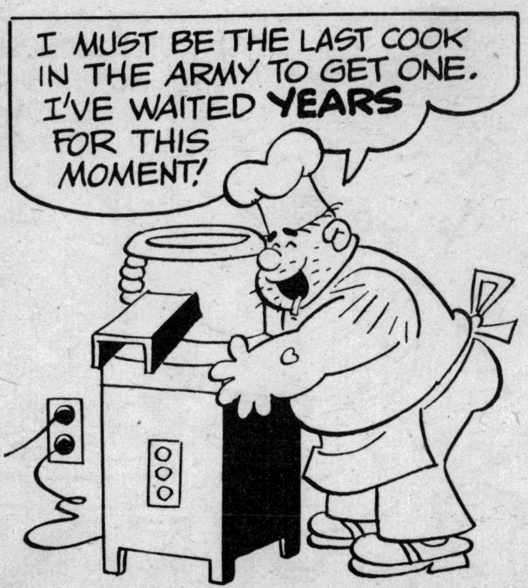
I MUST BE THE LAST COOK IN THE ARMY TO GET ONE. I'VE WAITED YEARS FOR THIS MOMENT!

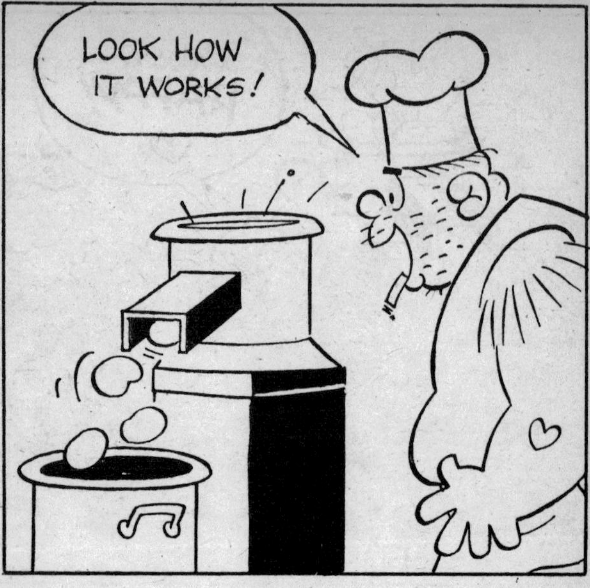
LOOK HOW IT WORKS!

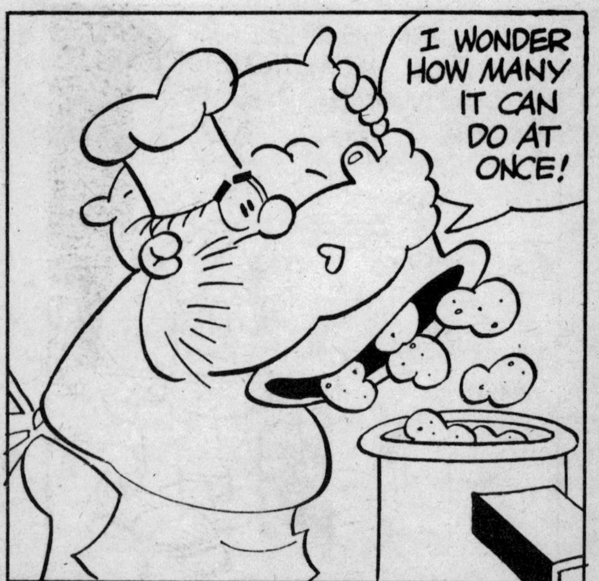
I WONDER HOW MANY IT CAN DO AT ONCE!

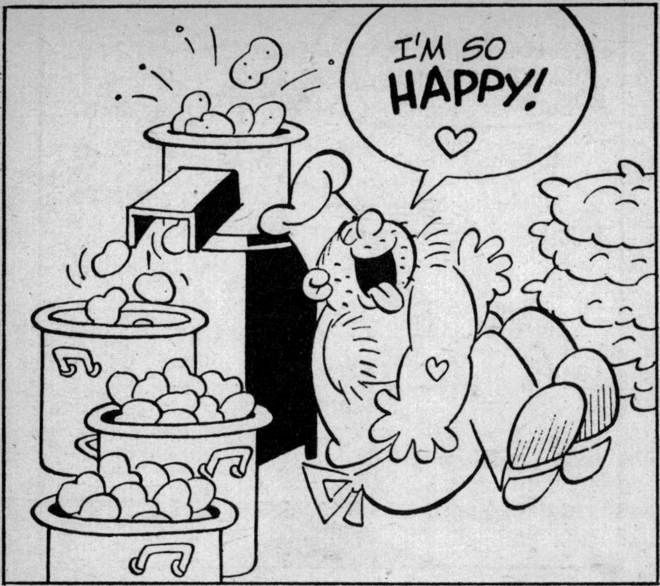
I'M SO HAPPY!

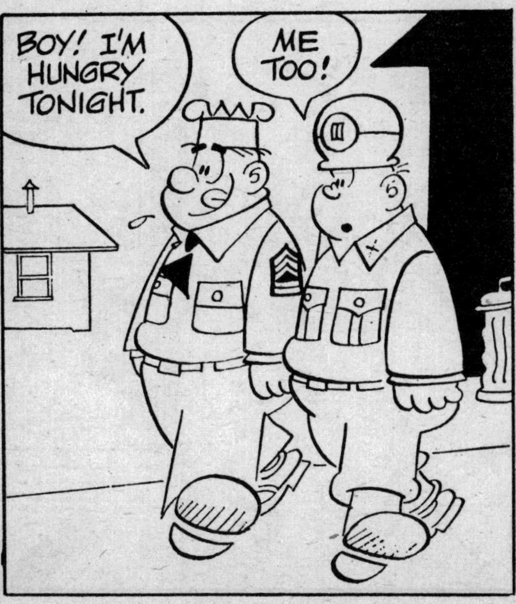
BOY! I'M HUNGRY TONIGHT.
ME TOO!

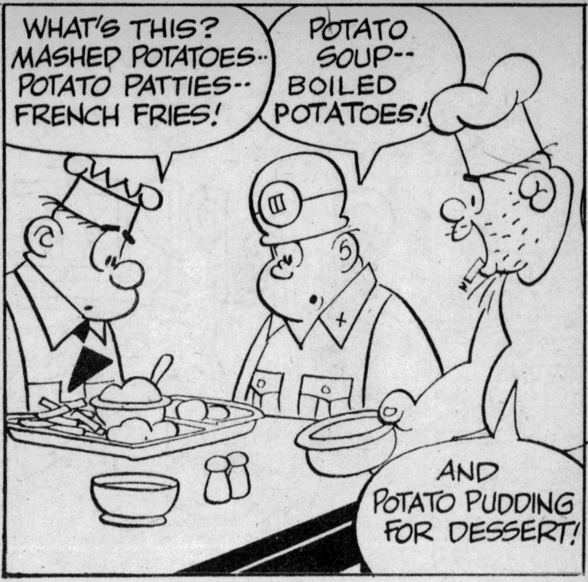
WHAT'S THIS? MASHED POTATOES.. POTATO PATTIES-- FRENCH FRIES!
POTATO SOUP-- BOILED POTATOES!
AND POTATO PUDDING FOR DESSERT!

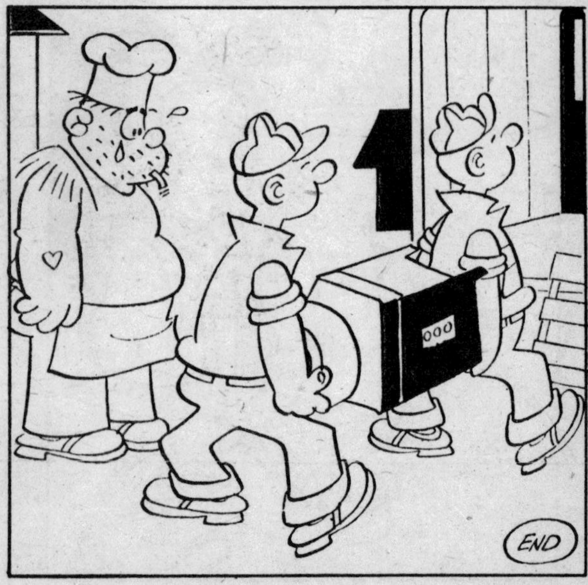
END

The SurPRIZE Winner

CAMP SWAMPY BOWLING LEAGUE
THIS YEAR'S TOP BOWLER IN THE OFFICER'S WIVES LEAGUE..... GLADYS GREENBRASS!
HOORAY!!
LET'S HEAR IT FOR GLADYS!
YAY!
CLAP
CLAP

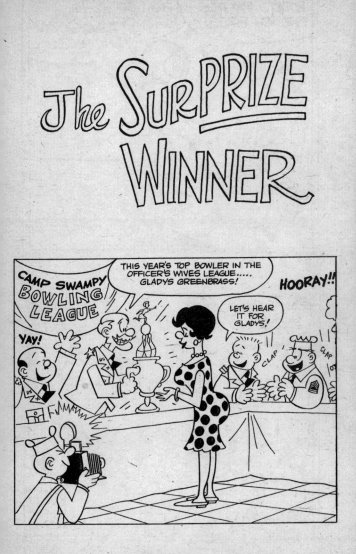

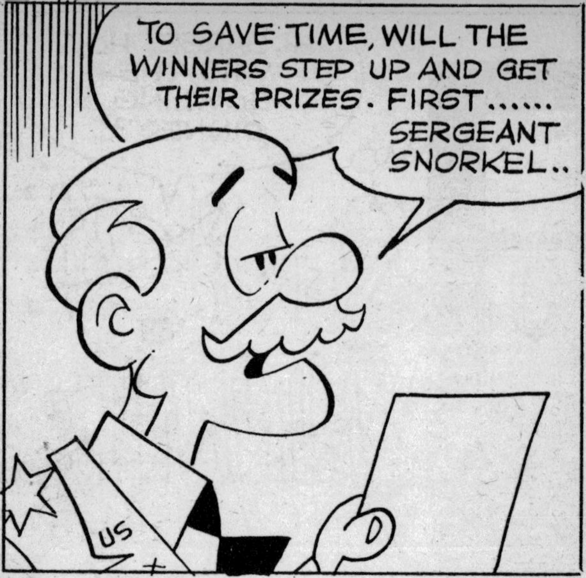
TO SAVE TIME, WILL THE WINNERS STEP UP AND GET THEIR PRIZES. FIRST...... SERGEANT SNORKEL..
US

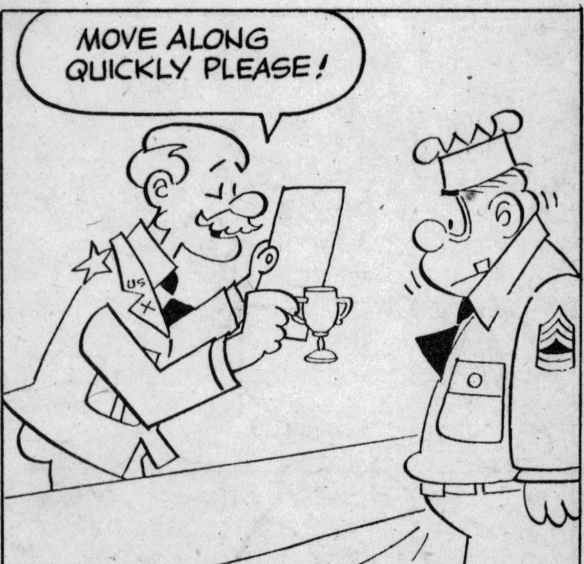
MOVE ALONG QUICKLY PLEASE!
US

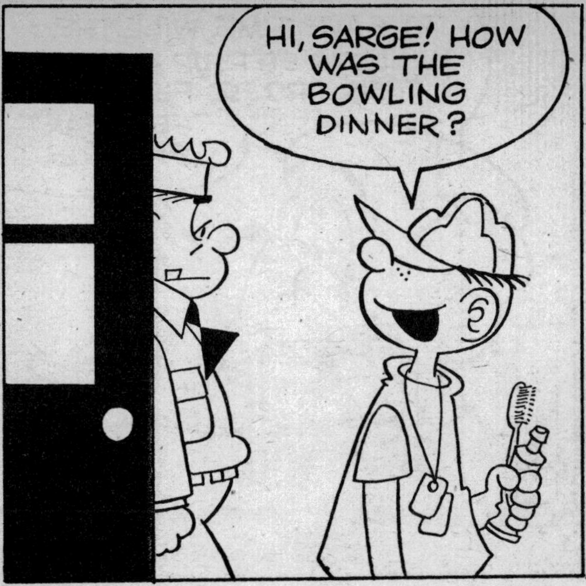
HI, SARGE! HOW WAS THE BOWLING DINNER?

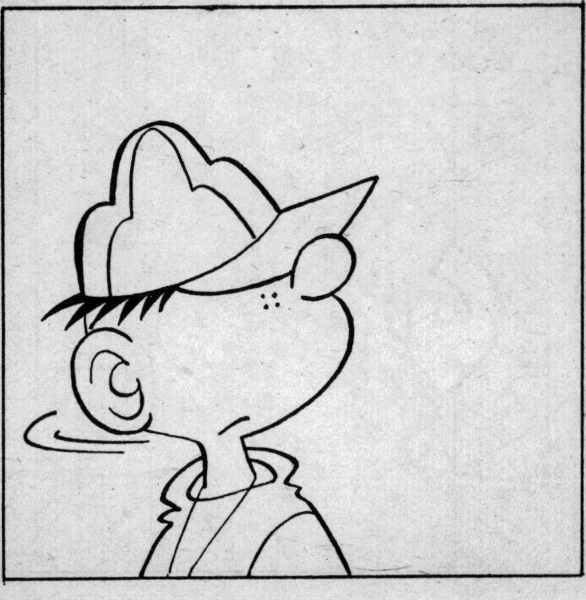

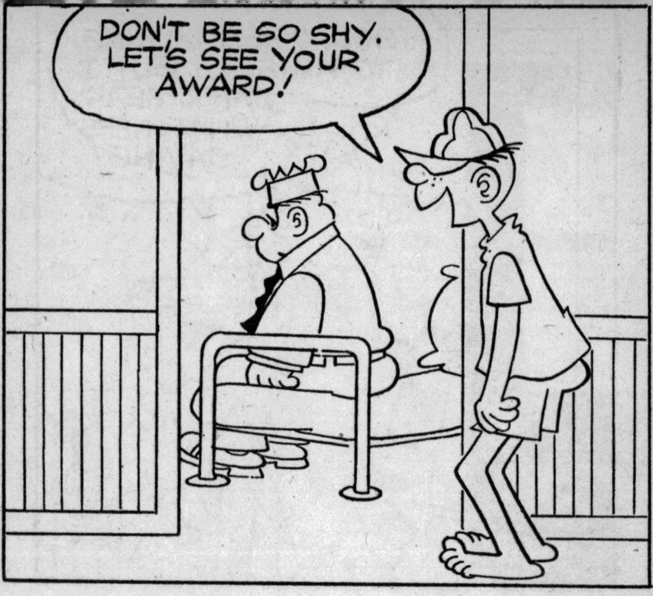
DON'T BE SO SHY. LET'S SEE YOUR AWARD!

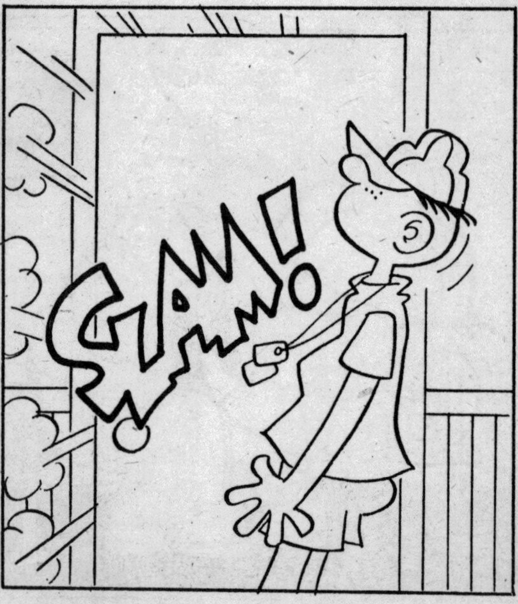
GAM!

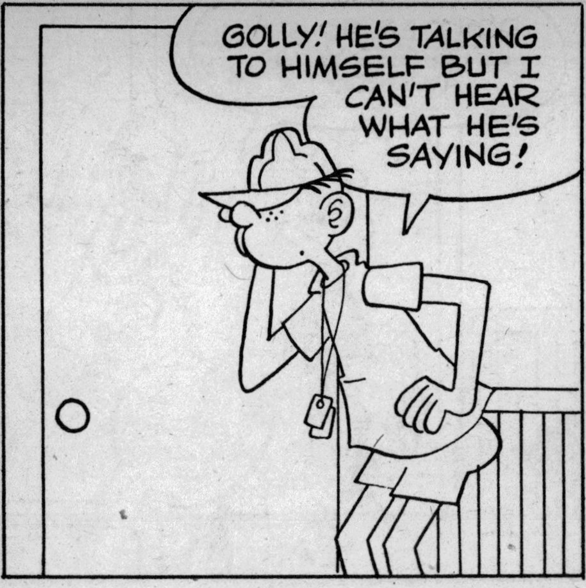
GOLLY! HE'S TALKING TO HIMSELF BUT I CAN'T HEAR WHAT HE'S SAYING!

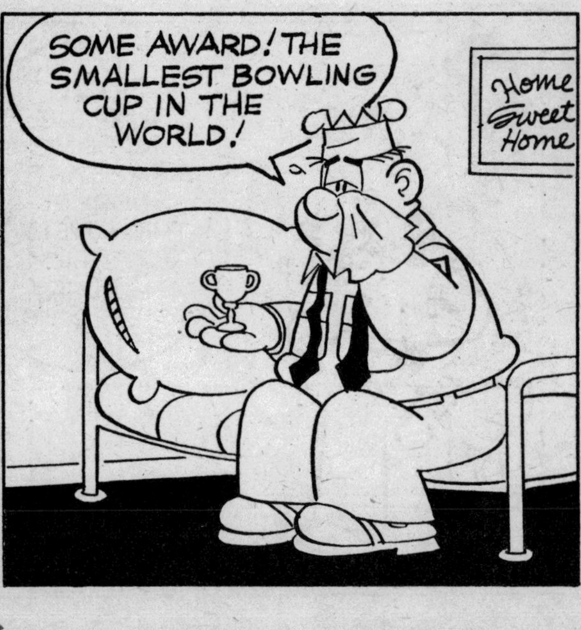
SOME AWARD! THE SMALLEST BOWLING CUP IN THE WORLD!
Home Sweet Home

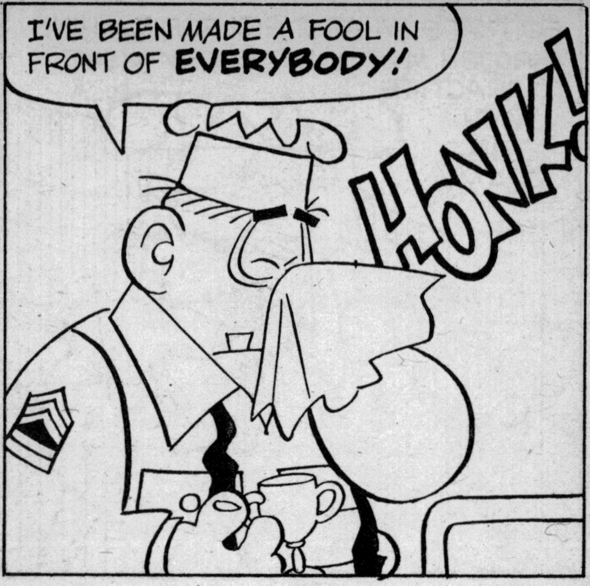
I'VE BEEN MADE A FOOL IN FRONT OF EVERYBODY!
HONK!

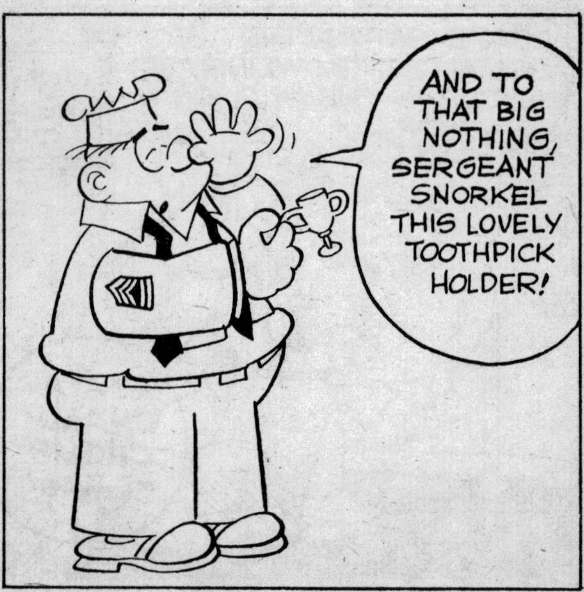
AND TO THAT BIG NOTHING, SERGEANT SNORKEL THIS LOVELY TOOTHPICK HOLDER!

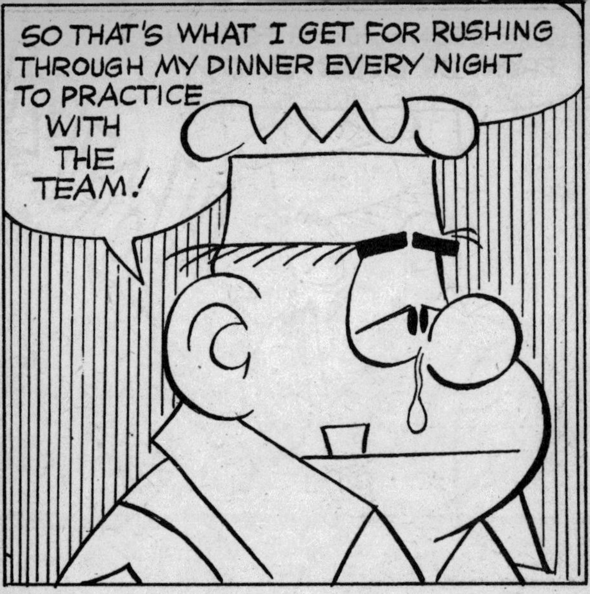
SO THAT'S WHAT I GET FOR RUSHING THROUGH MY DINNER EVERY NIGHT TO PRACTICE WITH THE TEAM!

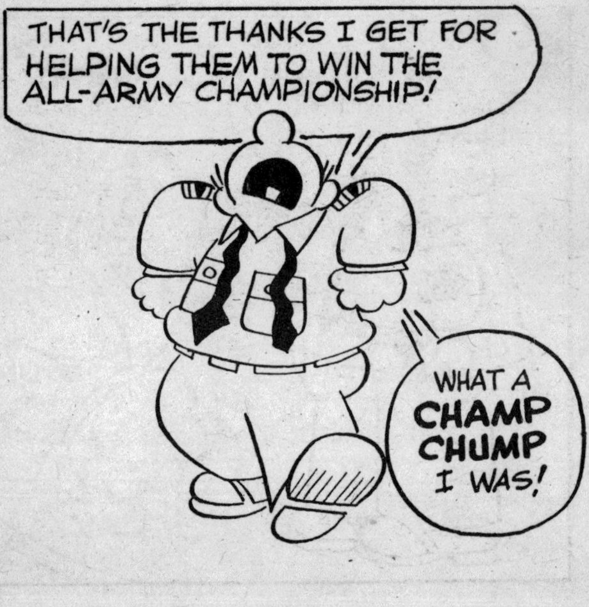
THAT'S THE THANKS I GET FOR HELPING THEM TO WIN THE ALL-ARMY CHAMPIONSHIP!
WHAT A CHAMP CHUMP I WAS!

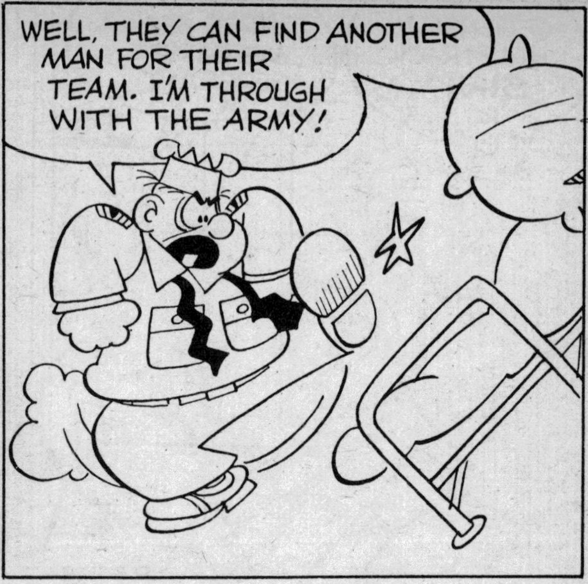
WELL, THEY CAN FIND ANOTHER MAN FOR THEIR TEAM. I'M THROUGH WITH THE ARMY!

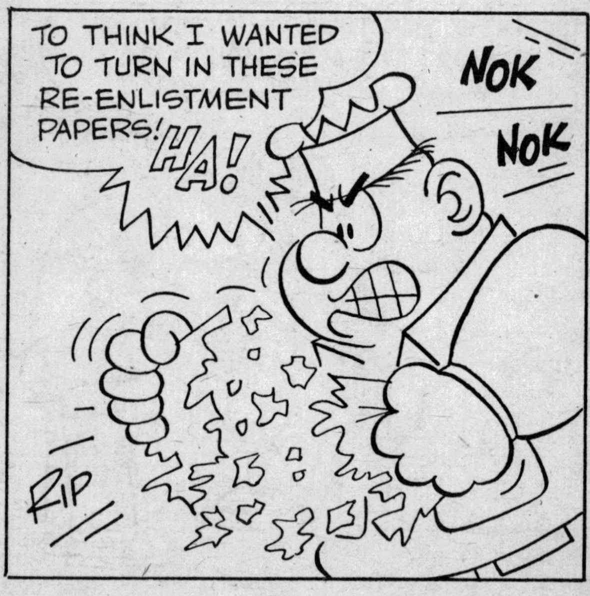
TO THINK I WANTED TO TURN IN THESE RE-ENLISTMENT PAPERS! HA!
NOK
NOK
RIP

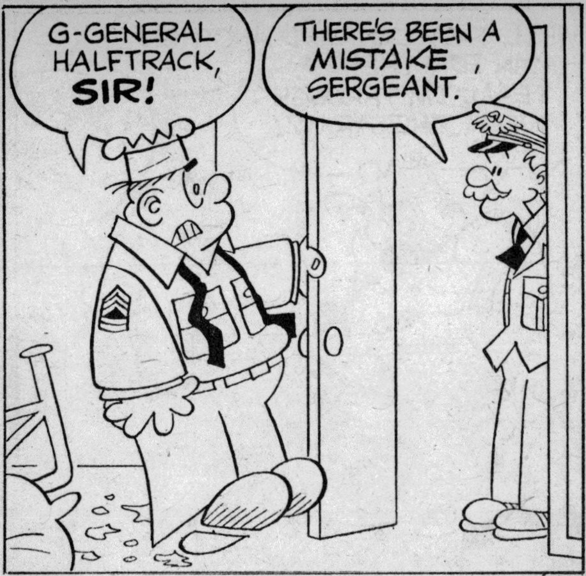
G-GENERAL HALFTRACK, SIR!
THERE'S BEEN A MISTAKE, SERGEANT.

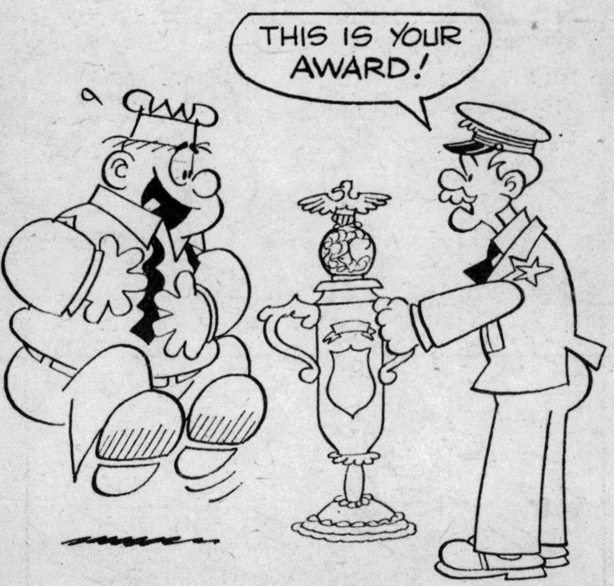
THIS IS YOUR AWARD!

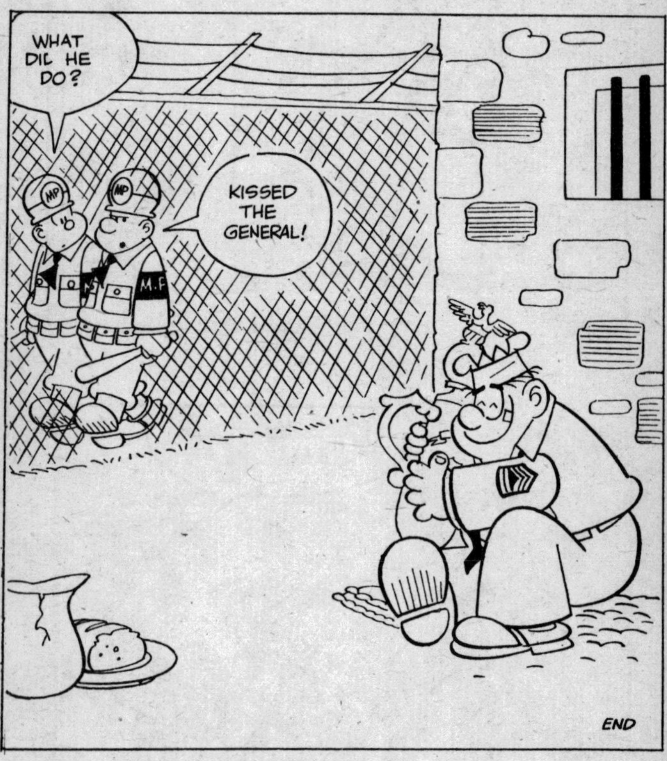
WHAT DID HE DO?
KISSED THE GENERAL!
MP
MP
M.P
END

TOUCH-UP ARTIST

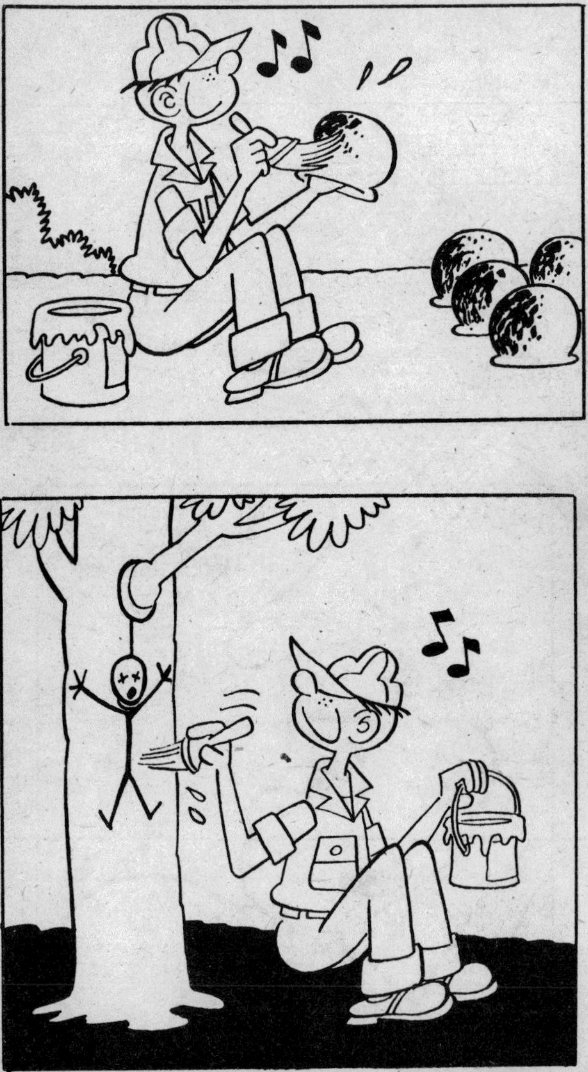

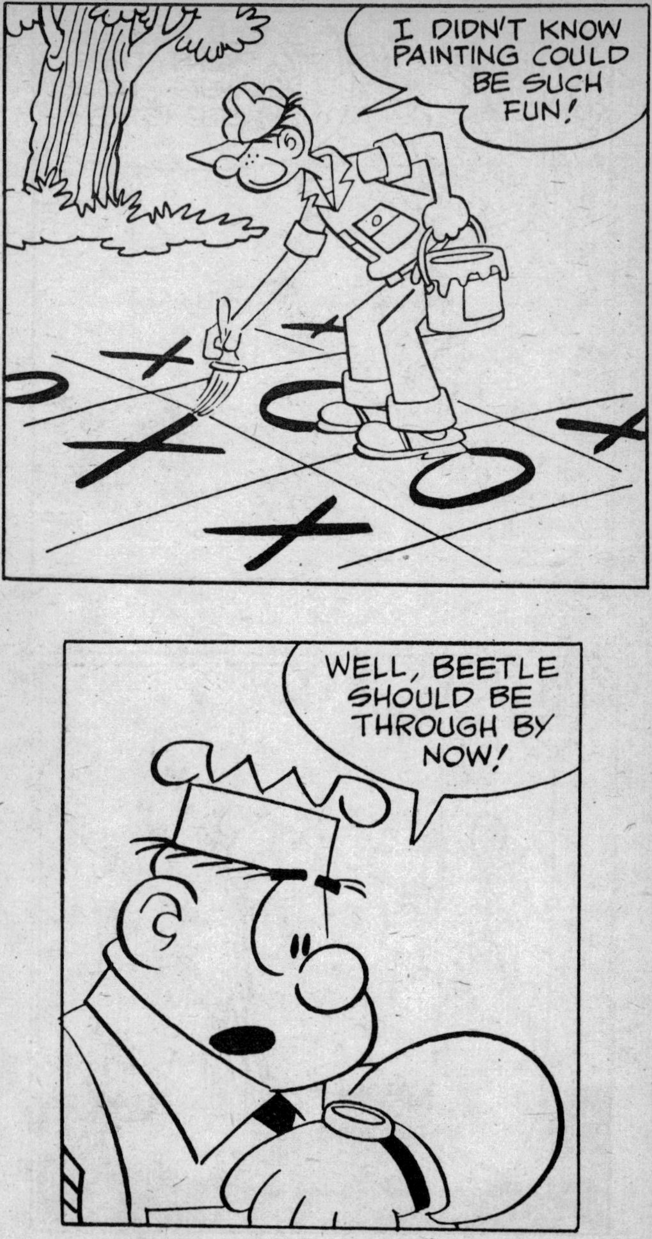
I DIDN'T KNOW PAINTING COULD BE SUCH FUN!
WELL, BEETLE SHOULD BE THROUGH BY NOW!

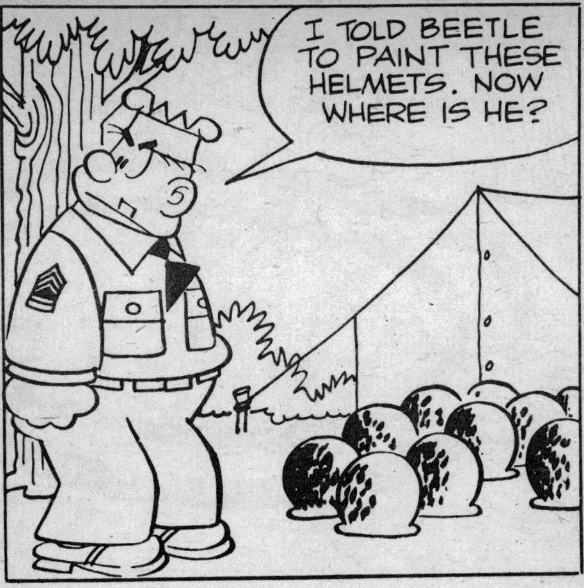
I TOLD BEETLE TO PAINT THESE HELMETS. NOW WHERE IS HE?

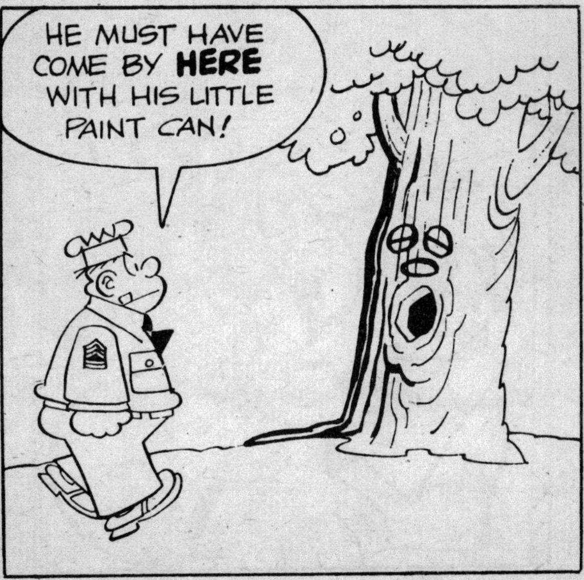
HE MUST HAVE COME BY **HERE** WITH HIS LITTLE PAINT CAN!

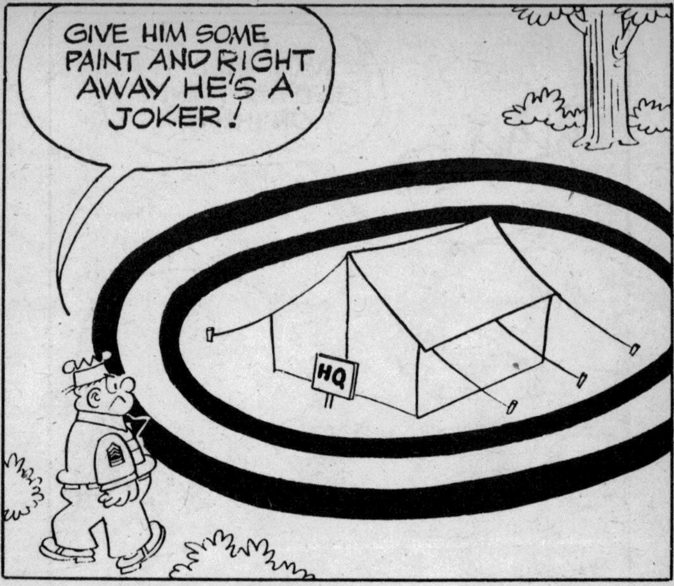
GIVE HIM SOME PAINT AND RIGHT AWAY HE'S A JOKER!
HQ

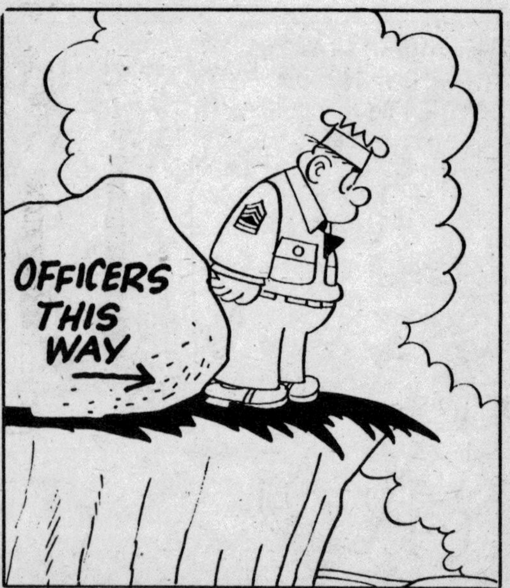
OFFICERS THIS WAY

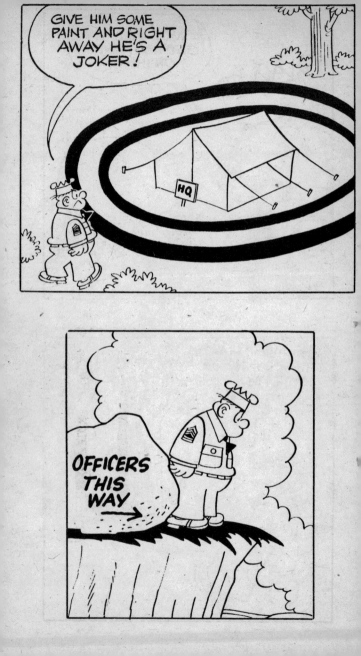

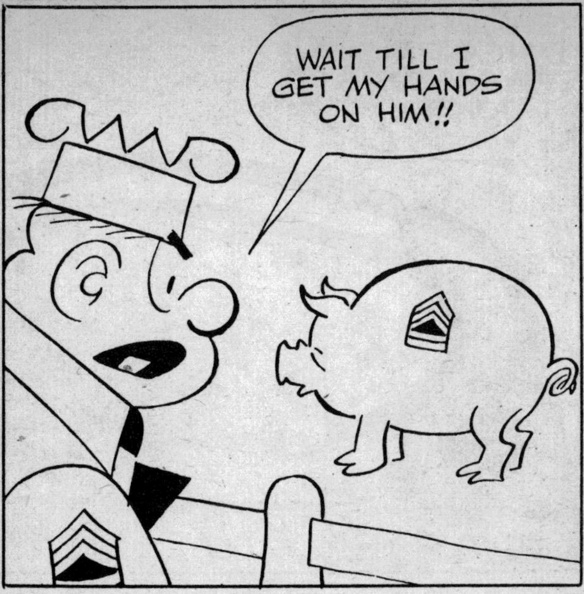
WAIT TILL I GET MY HANDS ON HIM!!

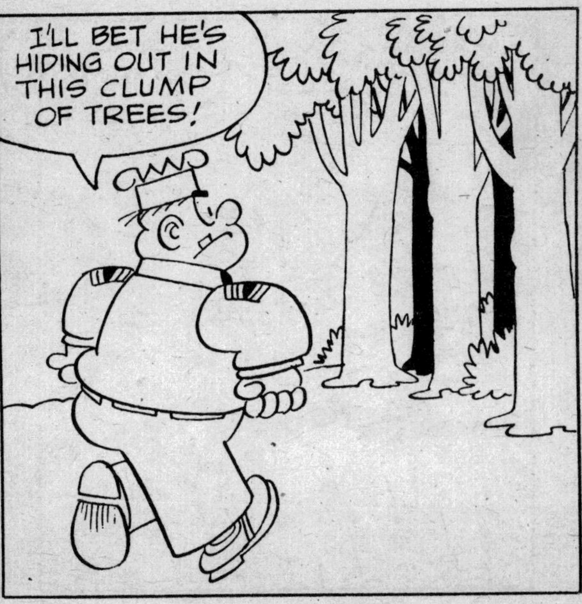
I'LL BET HE'S HIDING OUT IN THIS CLUMP OF TREES!

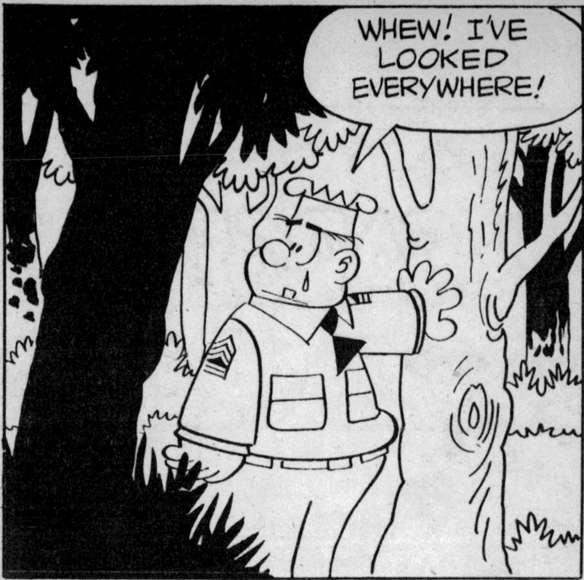
WHEW! I'VE LOOKED EVERYWHERE!

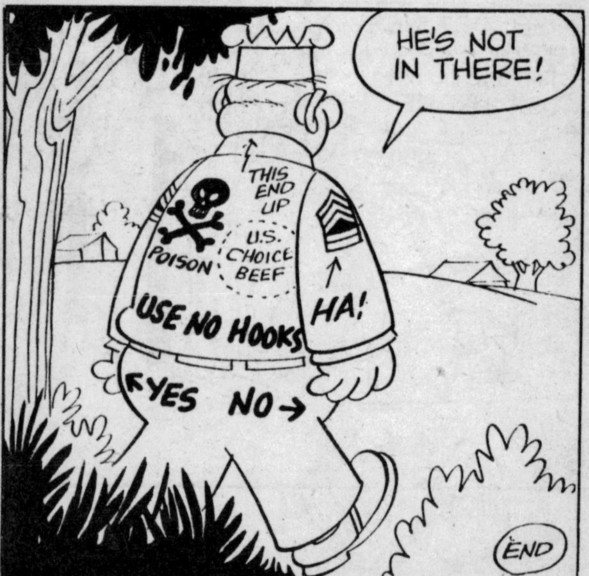
HE'S NOT IN THERE!
THIS END UP
POISON
U.S. CHOICE BEEF
USE NO HOOKS
HA!
YES
NO
END

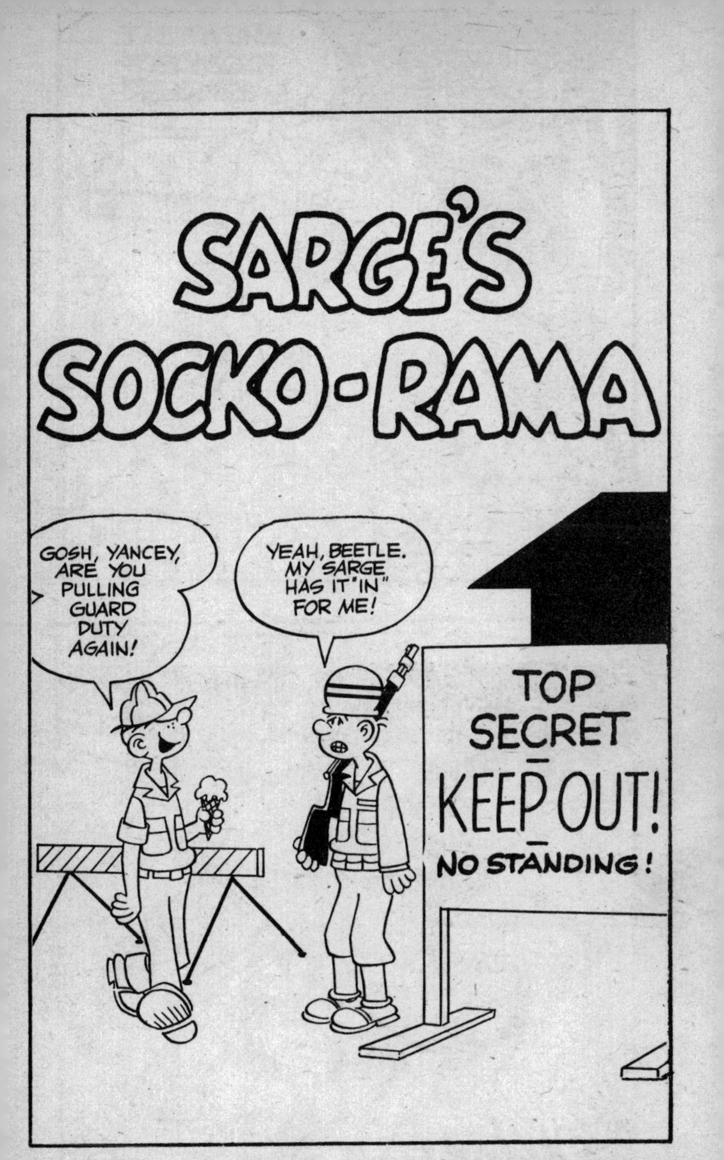
SARGE'S SOCKO-RAMA
GOSH, YANCEY, ARE YOU PULLING GUARD DUTY AGAIN!
YEAH, BEETLE. MY SARGE HAS IT "IN" FOR ME!
TOP SECRET
KEEP OUT!
NO STANDING!

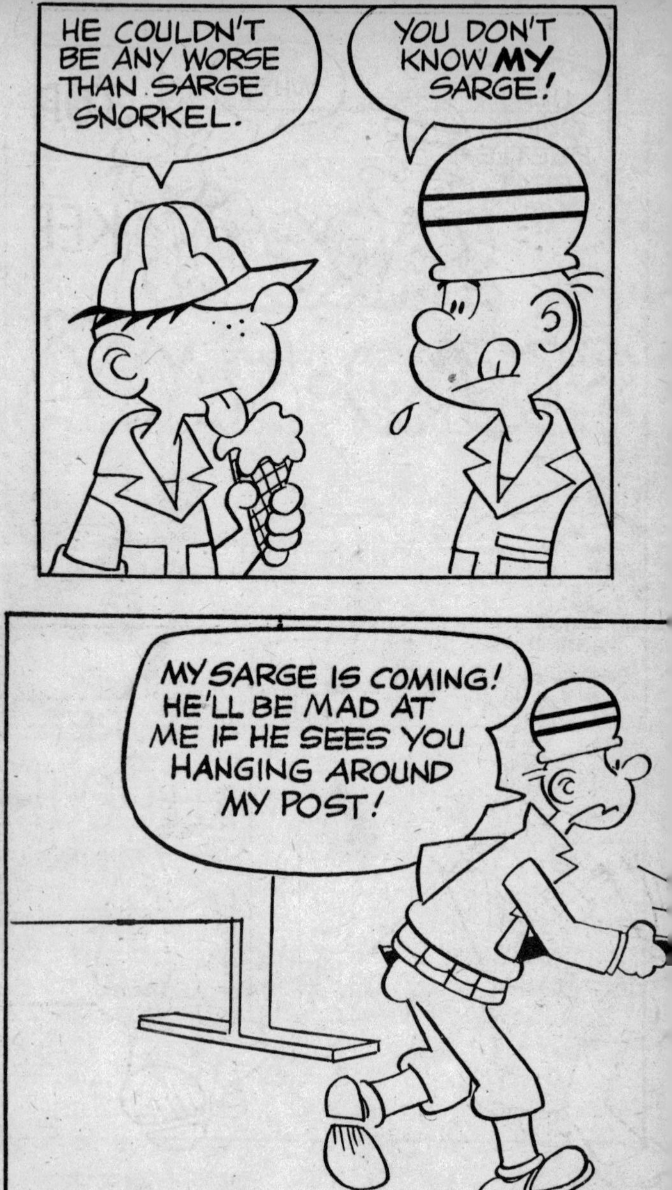
HE COULDN'T BE ANY WORSE THAN SARGE SNORKEL.
YOU DON'T KNOW **MY** SARGE!
MY SARGE IS COMING! HE'LL BE MAD AT ME IF HE SEES YOU HANGING AROUND MY POST!

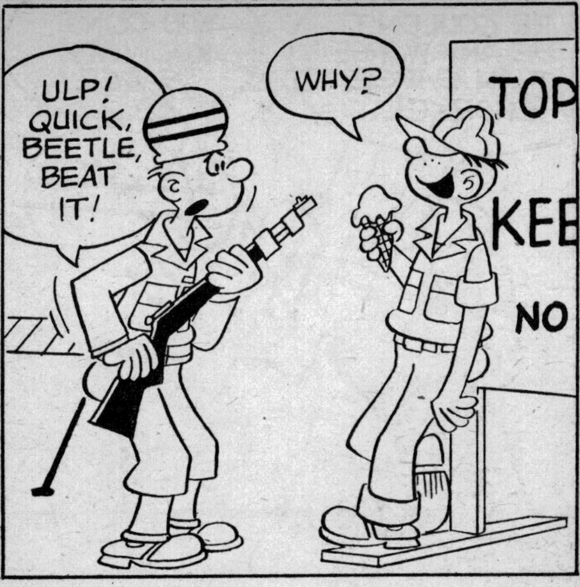
ULP! QUICK, BEETLE, BEAT IT!
WHY?
TOP
KEE
NO

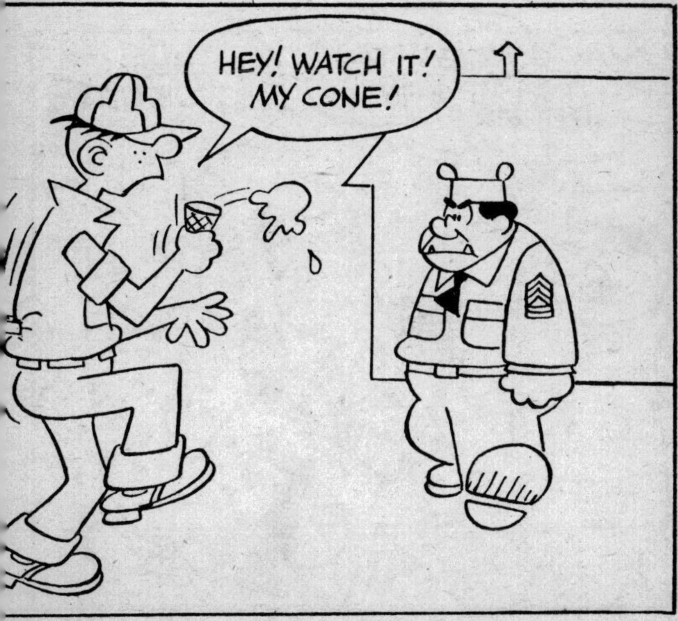
HEY! WATCH IT! MY CONE!

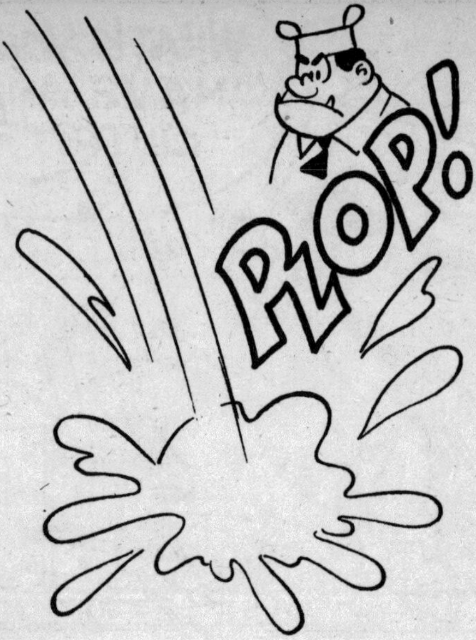
PLOP!

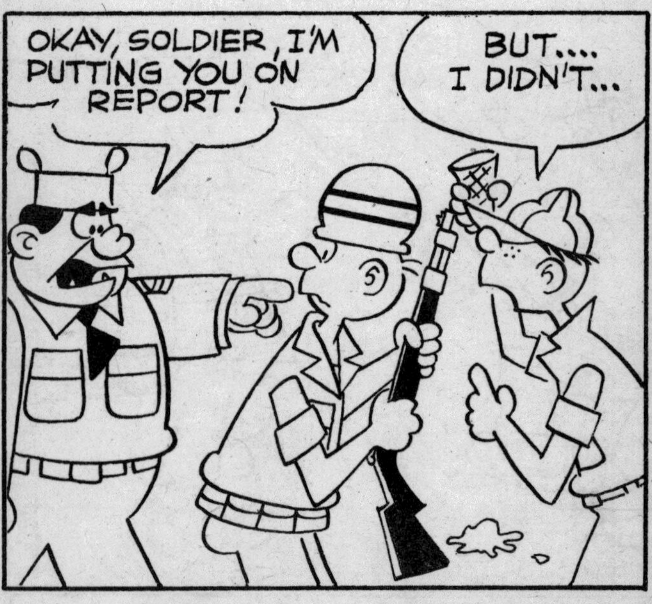
OKAY, SOLDIER, I'M PUTTING YOU ON REPORT!
BUT.... I DIDN'T...

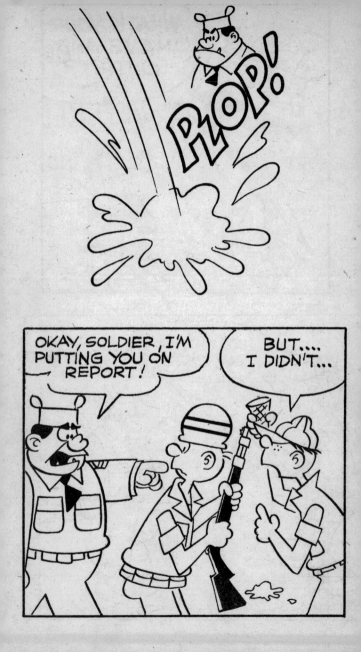

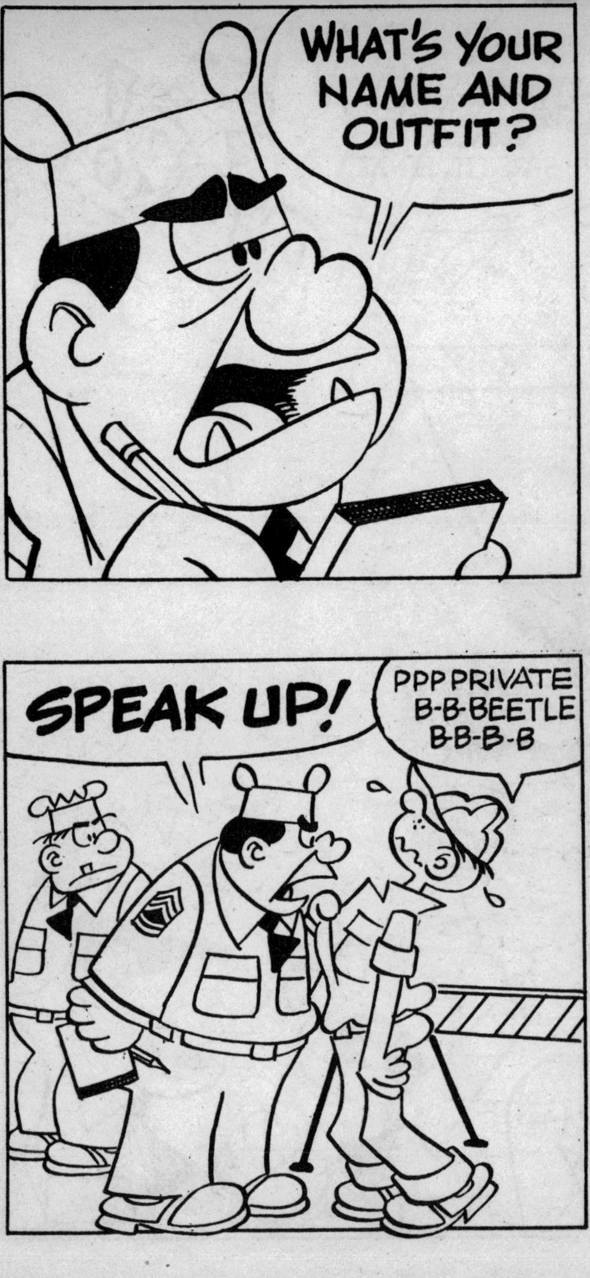
WHAT'S YOUR NAME AND OUTFIT?
SPEAK UP!
PPP PRIVATE B-B-BEETLE B-B-B-B

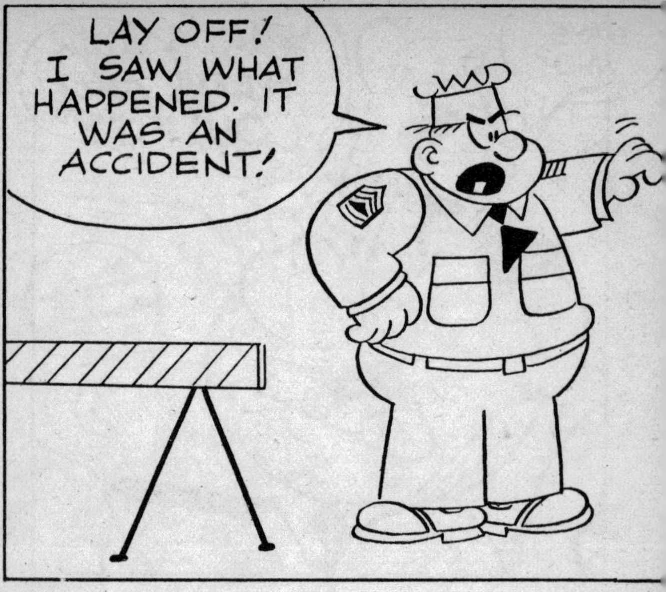
LAY OFF! I SAW WHAT HAPPENED. IT WAS AN ACCIDENT!

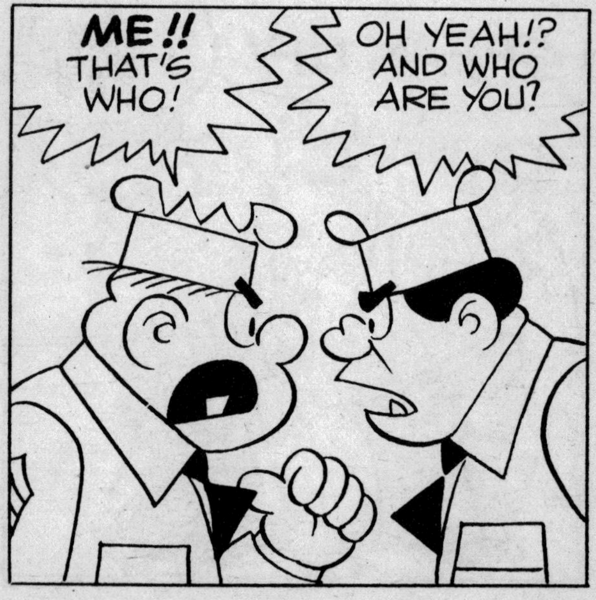
OH YEAH!? AND WHO ARE YOU?
ME!! THAT'S WHO!

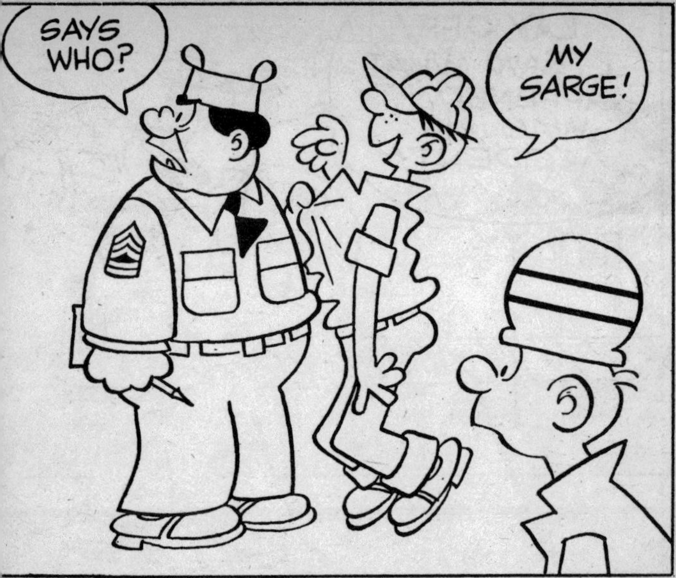
SAYS WHO?
MY SARGE!

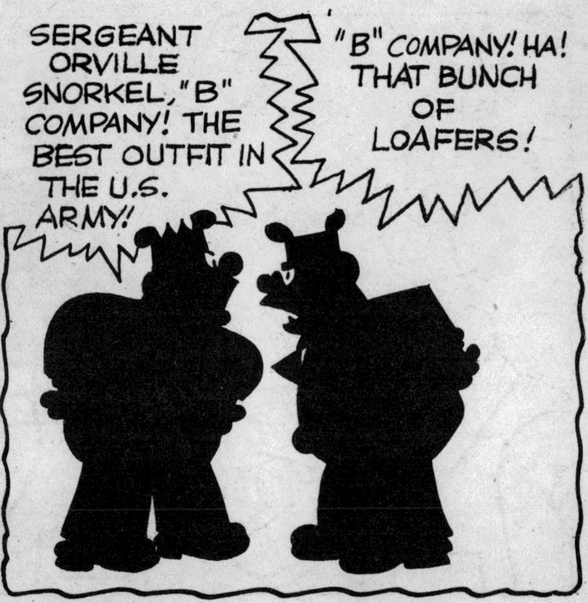
SERGEANT ORVILLE SNORKEL, "B" COMPANY! THE BEST OUTFIT IN THE U.S. ARMY!
"B" COMPANY! HA! THAT BUNCH OF LOAFERS!

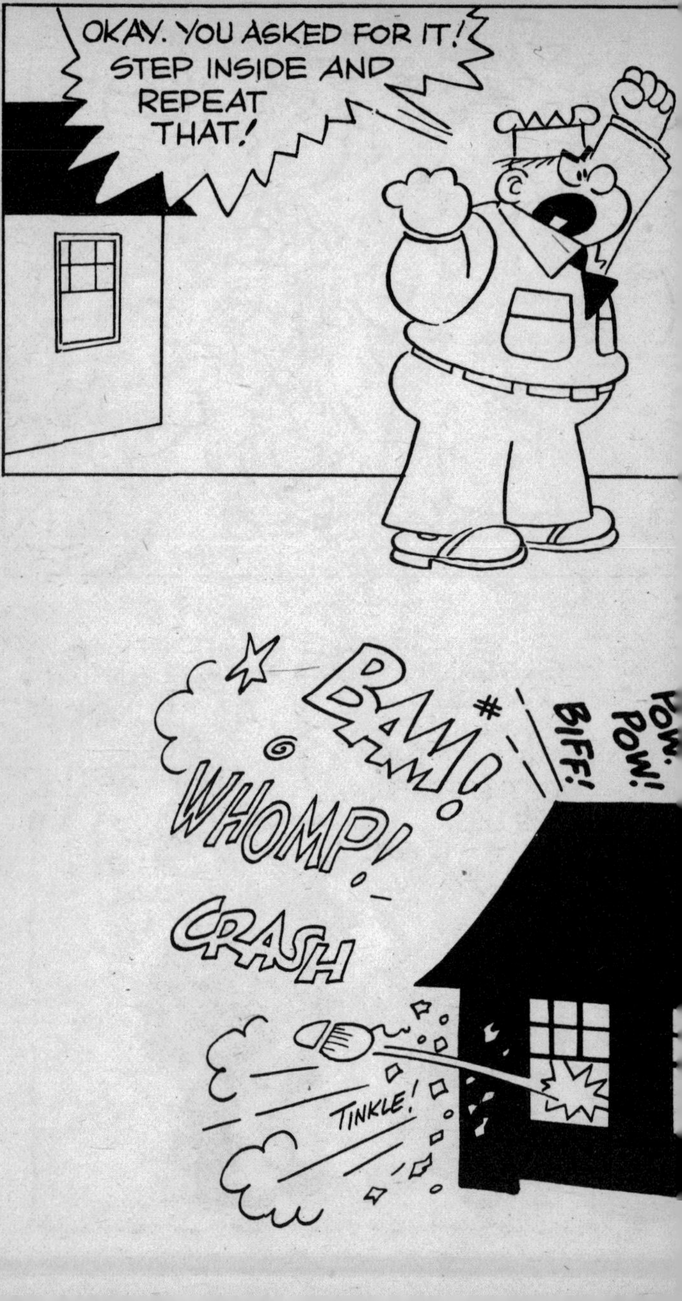
OKAY. YOU ASKED FOR IT!
STEP INSIDE AND
REPEAT
THAT!
BAM!
WHOMP!
CRASH
BIFF!
POW! POW!
TINKLE!

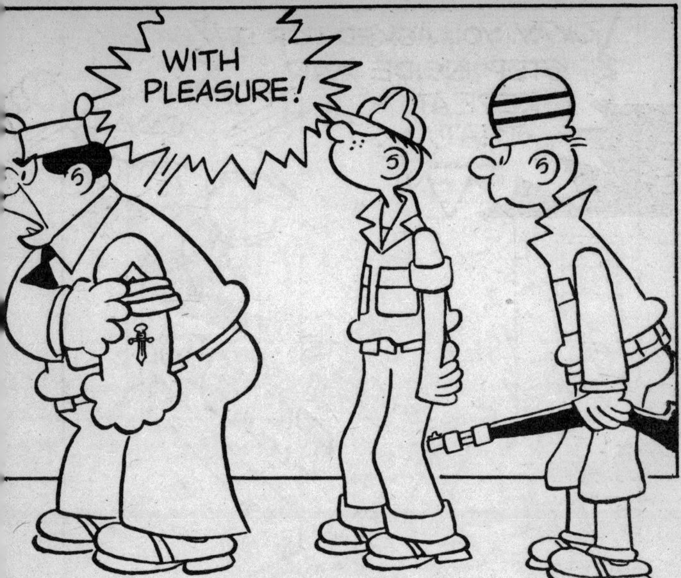
WITH PLEASURE!

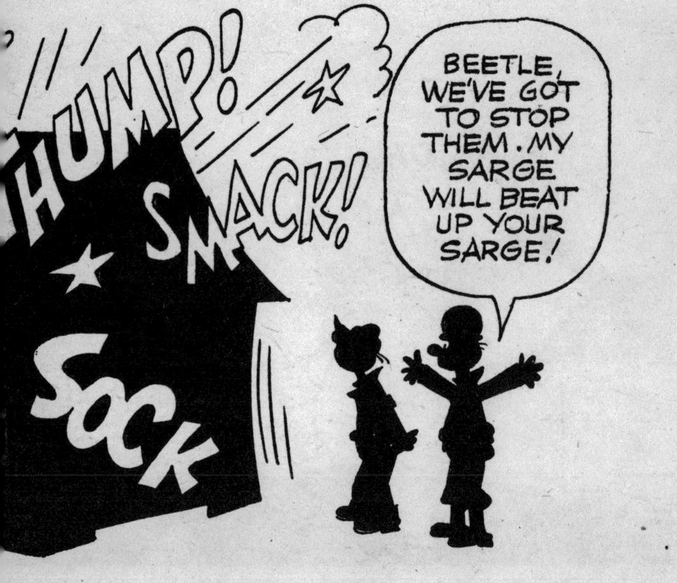
HUMP!
SMACK!
SOCK
BEETLE, WE'VE GOT TO STOP THEM. MY SARGE WILL BEAT UP YOUR SARGE!

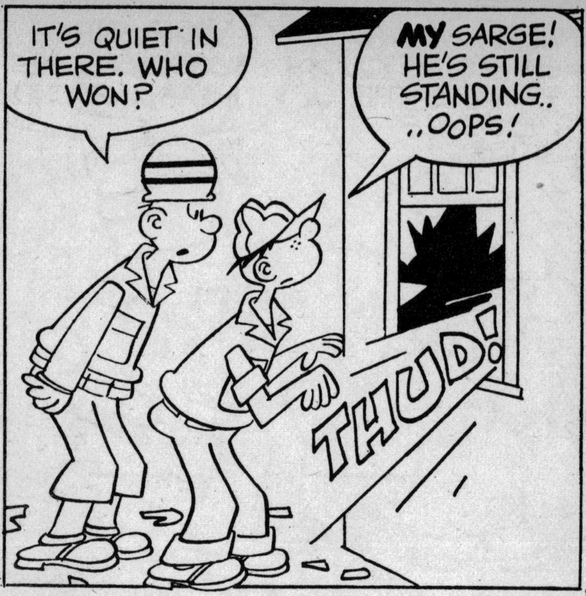
IT'S QUIET IN THERE. WHO WON?
MY SARGE! HE'S STILL STANDING.. ..OOPS!
THUD!

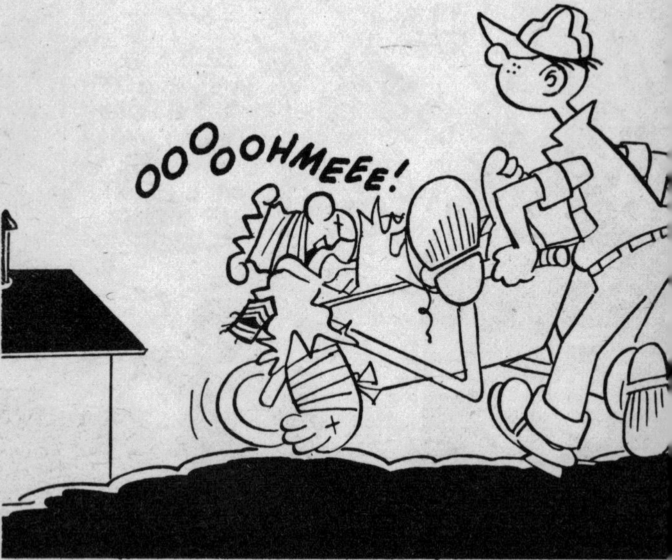
OOOOOOHMEEEE!

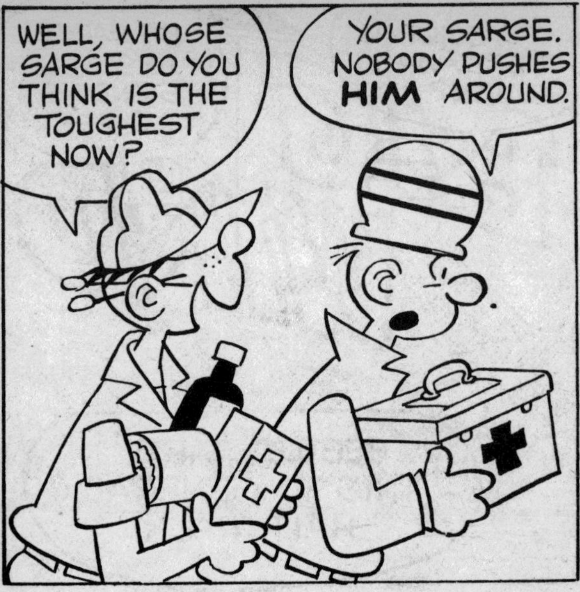
WELL, WHOSE SARGE DO YOU THINK IS THE TOUGHEST NOW?
YOUR SARGE. NOBODY PUSHES HIM AROUND.

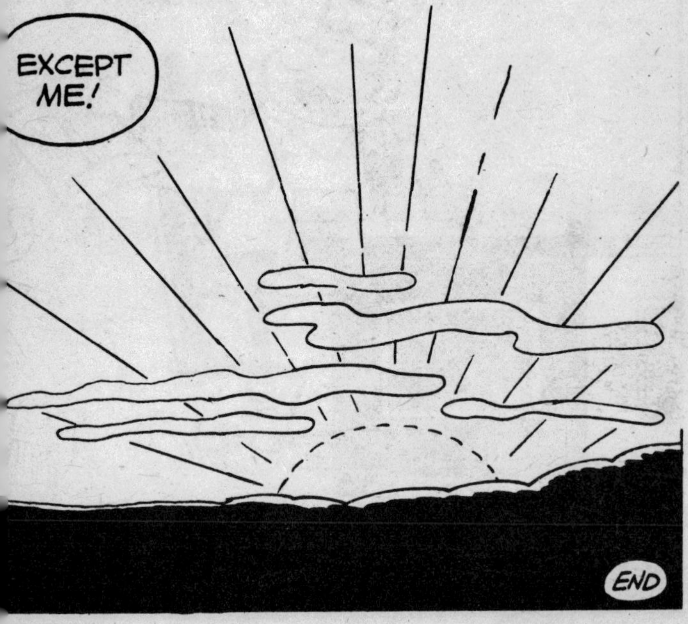
EXCEPT ME!
END

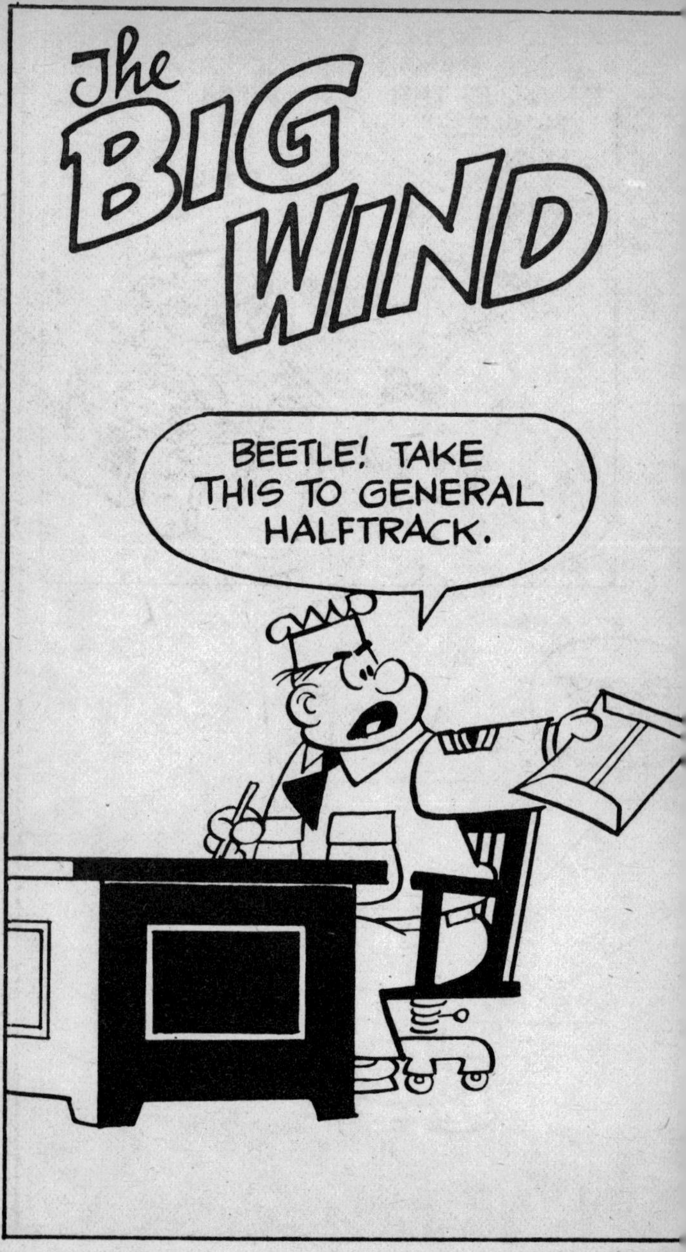
The BIG WIND
BEETLE! TAKE THIS TO GENERAL HALFTRACK.

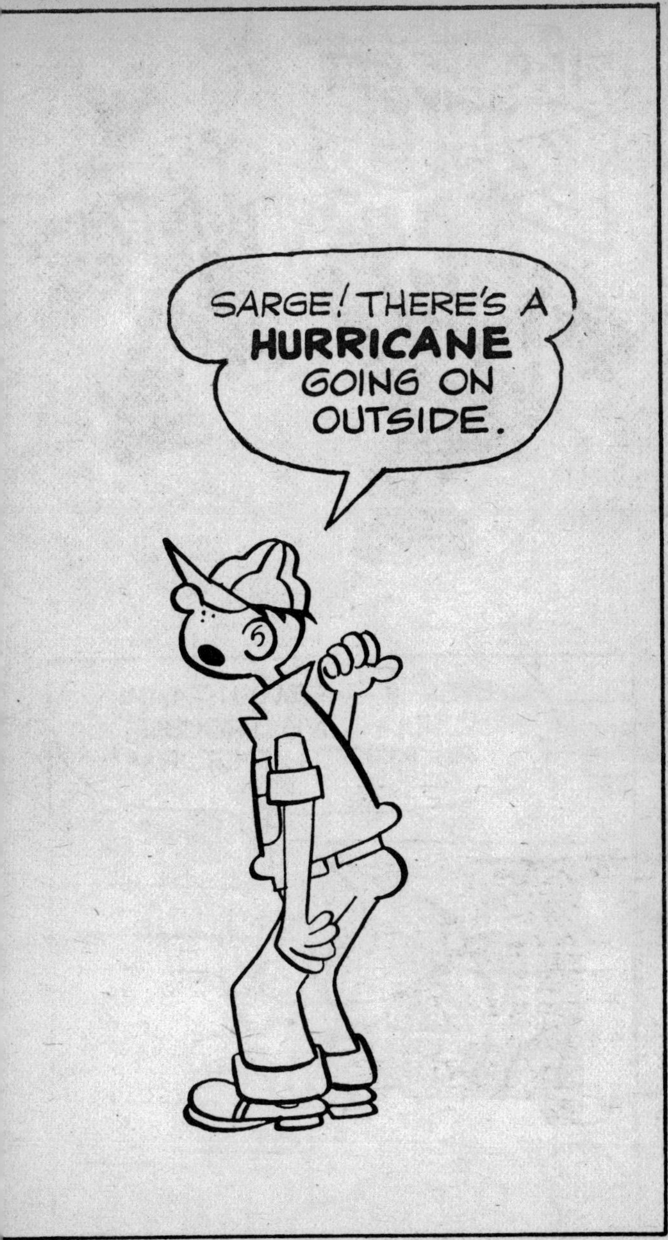
SARGE! THERE'S A **HURRICANE** GOING ON OUTSIDE.

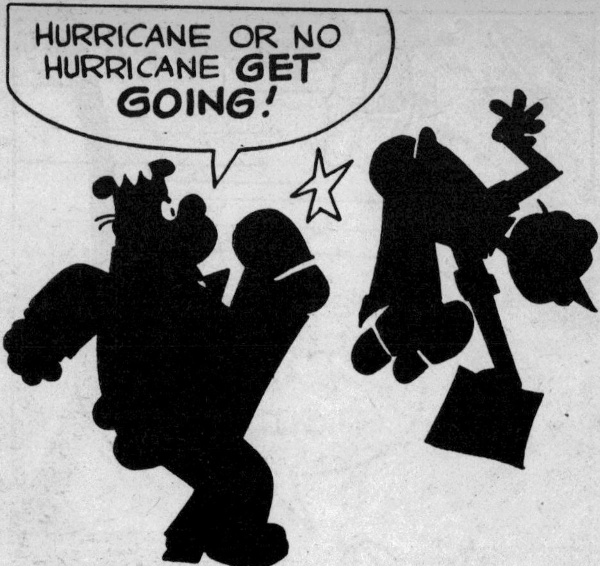
HURRICANE OR NO HURRICANE GET GOING!

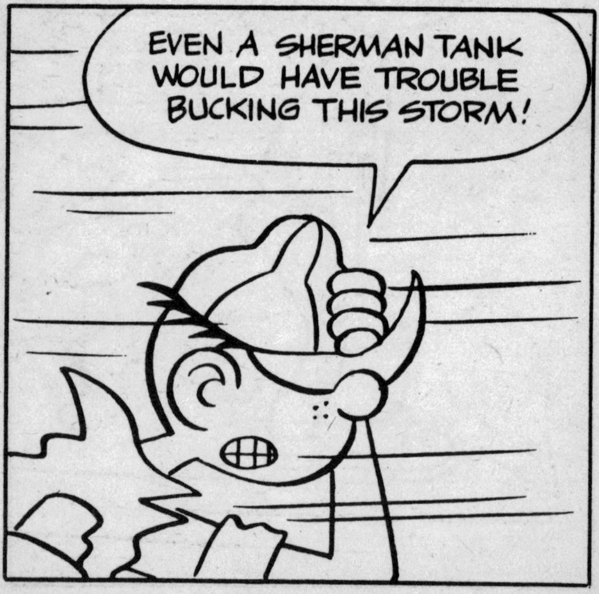
EVEN A SHERMAN TANK WOULD HAVE TROUBLE BUCKING THIS STORM!

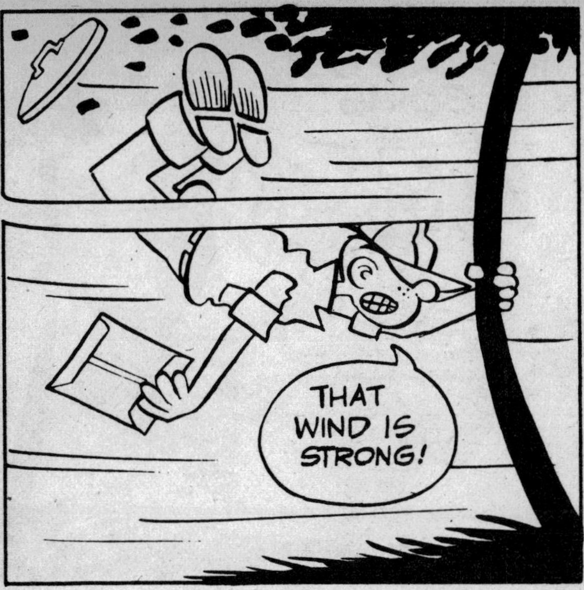
THAT WIND IS STRONG!

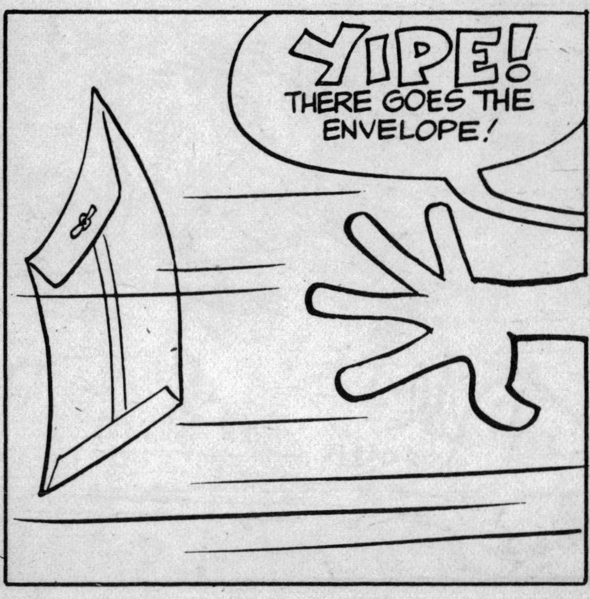
YIPE!
THERE GOES THE ENVELOPE!

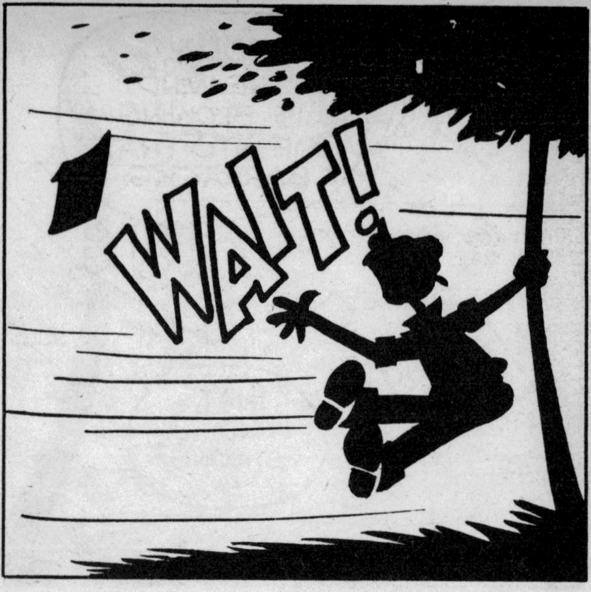
WAIT!

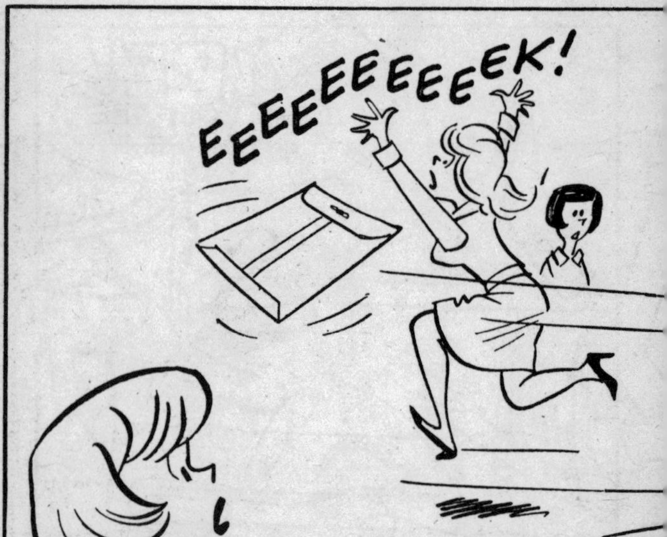
EEEEEEEEEEEEK!

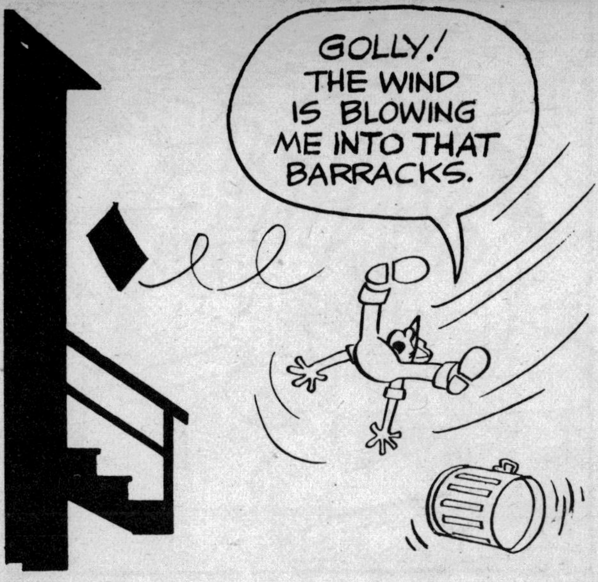
GOLLY! THE WIND IS BLOWING ME INTO THAT BARRACKS.

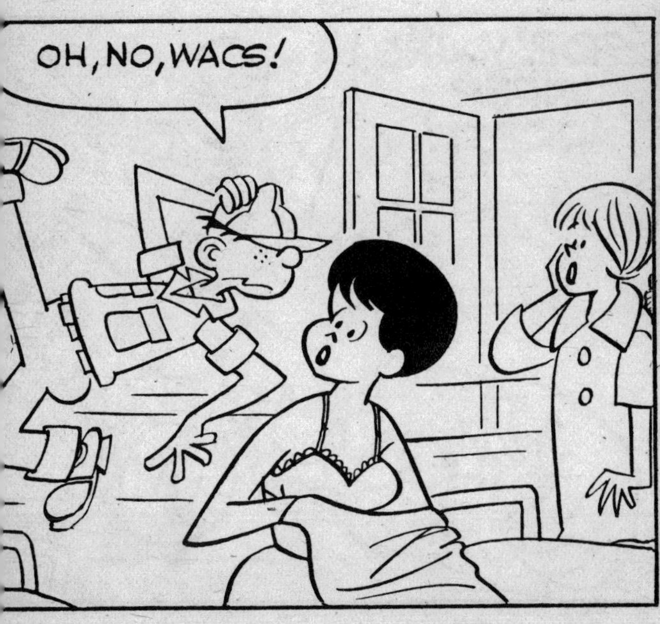
OH, NO, WACS!

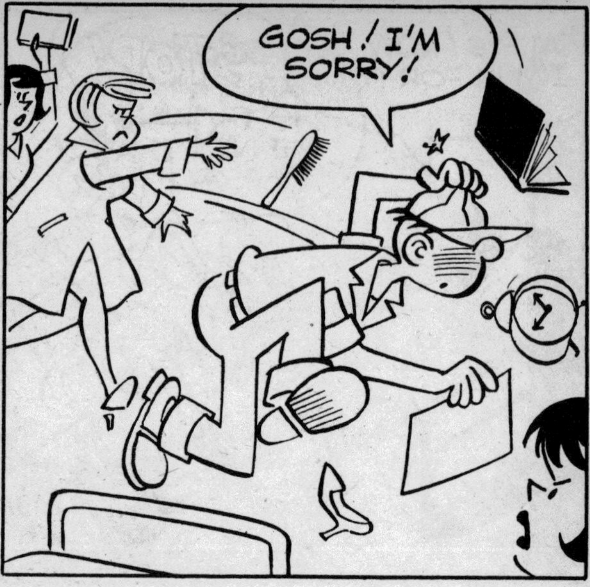
GOSH! I'M SORRY!

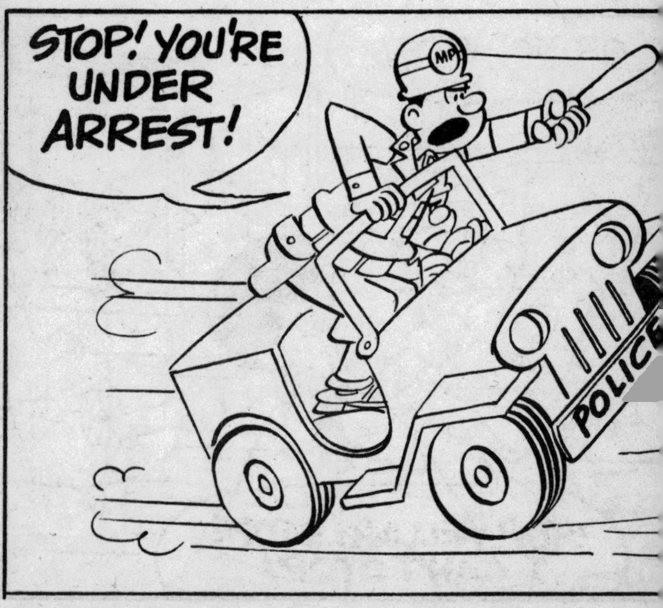
STOP! YOU'RE UNDER ARREST!

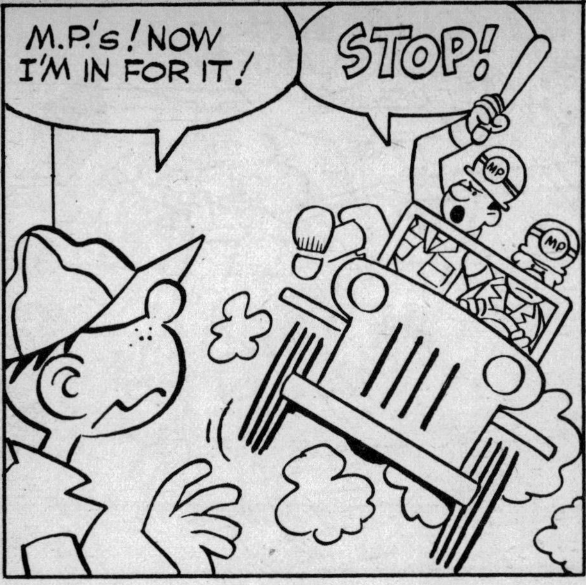
M.P.'s! NOW I'M IN FOR IT!
STOP!
MP
MP

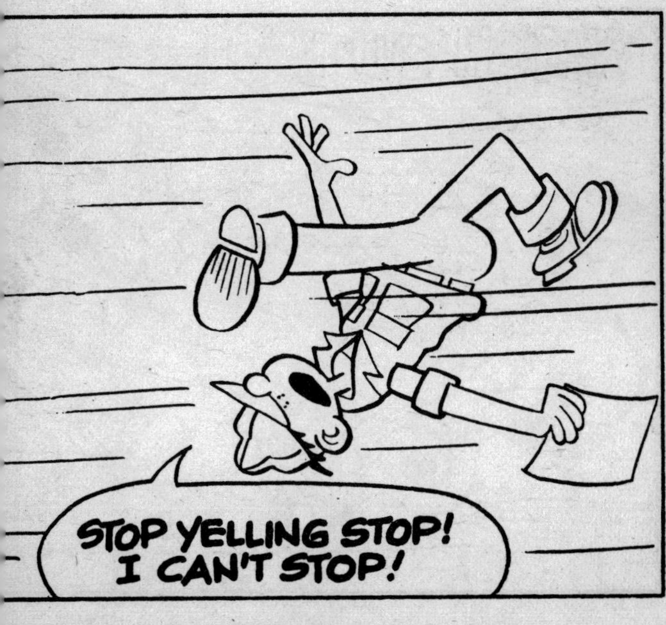
STOP YELLING STOP! I CAN'T STOP!

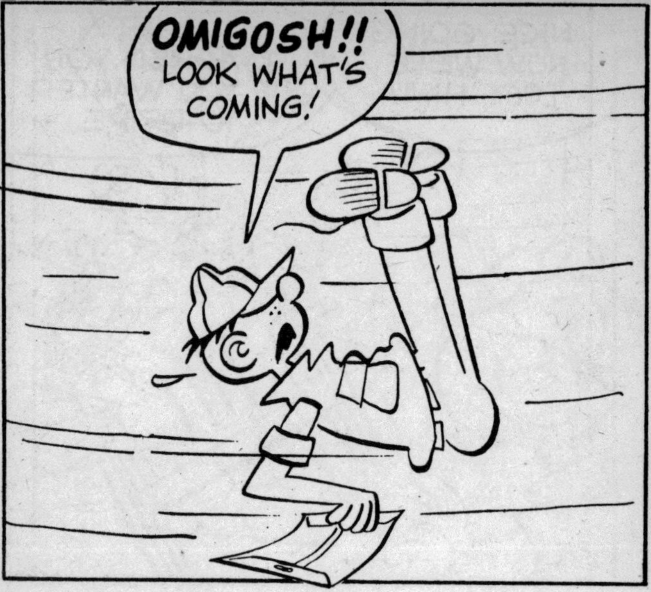
OMIGOSH!! LOOK WHAT'S COMING!

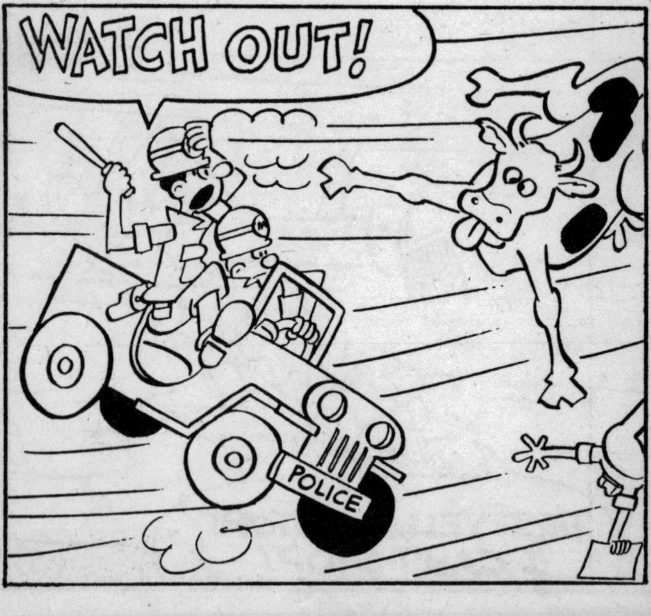
WATCH OUT!
POLICE

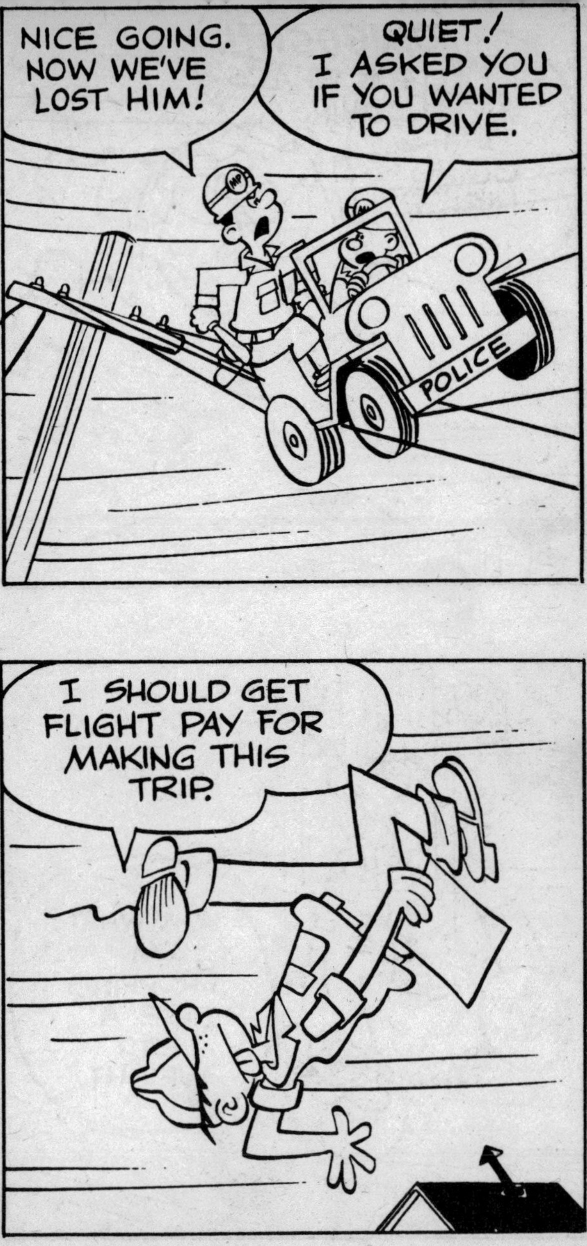
NICE GOING. NOW WE'VE LOST HIM!
QUIET! I ASKED YOU IF YOU WANTED TO DRIVE.
POLICE
I SHOULD GET FLIGHT PAY FOR MAKING THIS TRIP.

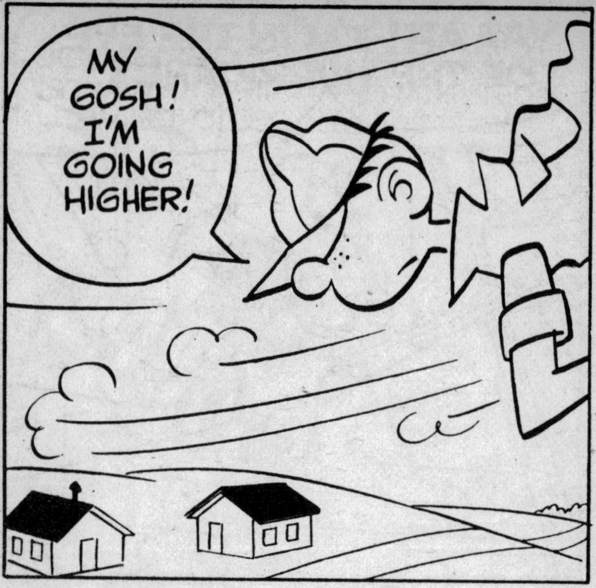
MY GOSH! I'M GOING HIGHER!

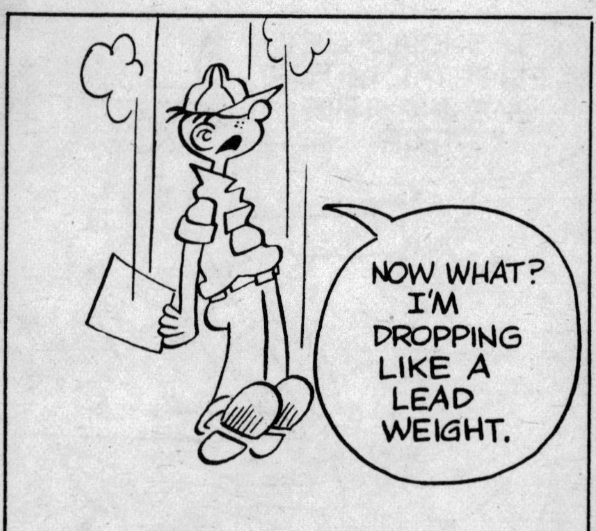
NOW WHAT? I'M DROPPING LIKE A LEAD WEIGHT.

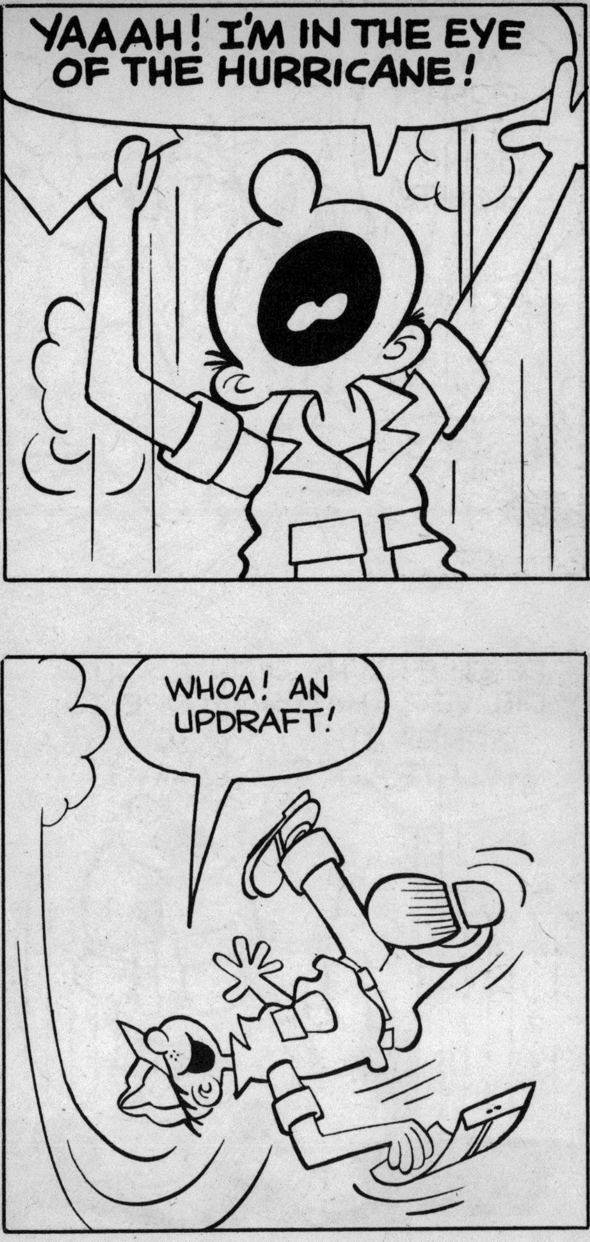
YAAAH! I'M IN THE EYE OF THE HURRICANE!
WHOA! AN UPDRAFT!

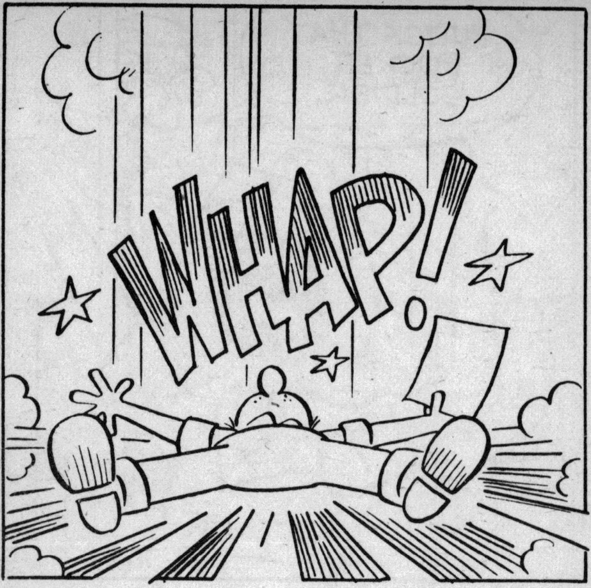
WHAP!

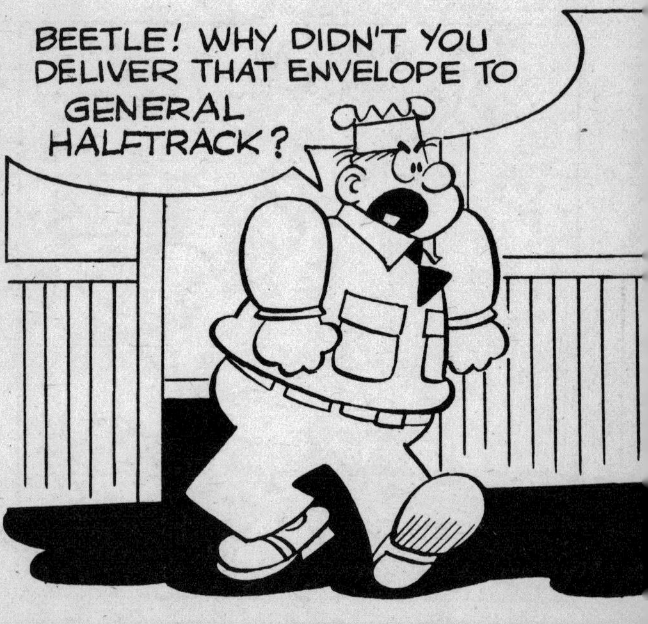
BEETLE! WHY DIDN'T YOU DELIVER THAT ENVELOPE TO GENERAL HALFTRACK?

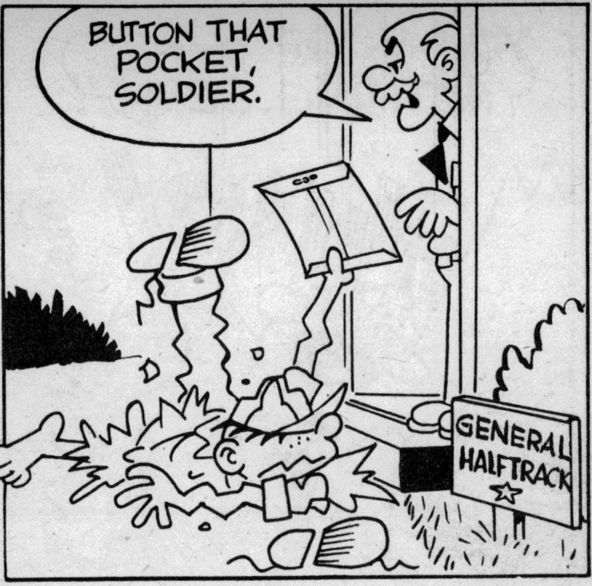
BUTTON THAT POCKET, SOLDIER.
GENERAL HALFTRACK

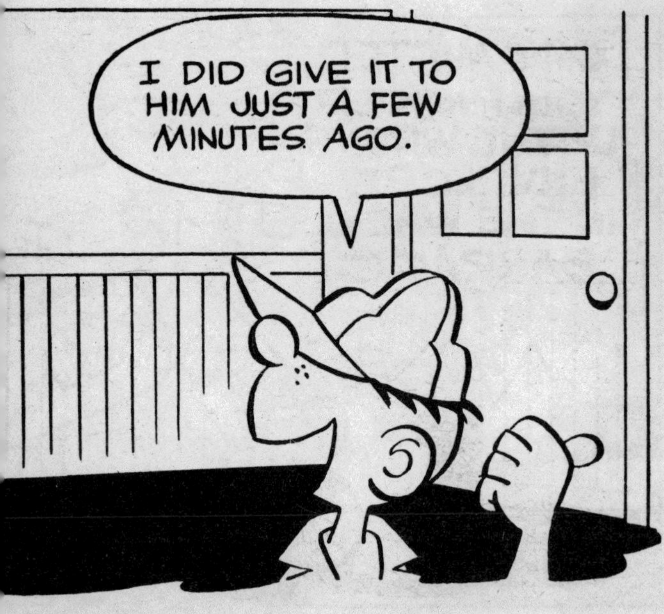
I DID GIVE IT TO HIM JUST A FEW MINUTES AGO.

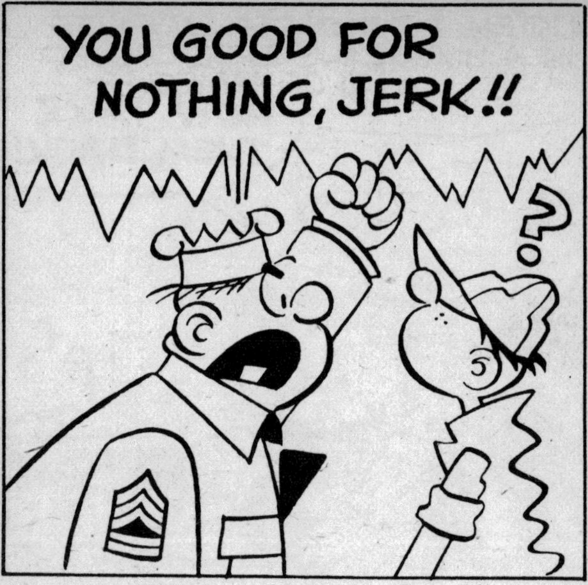
YOU GOOD FOR NOTHING, JERK!!
?

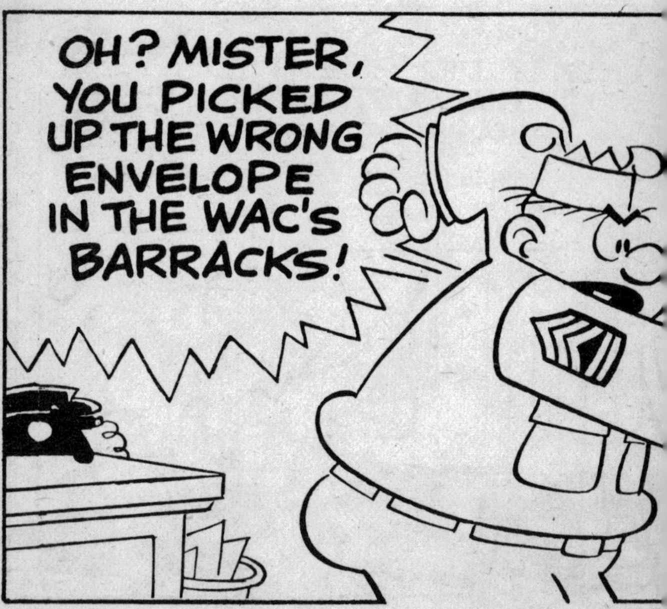
OH? MISTER, YOU PICKED UP THE WRONG ENVELOPE IN THE WAC'S BARRACKS!

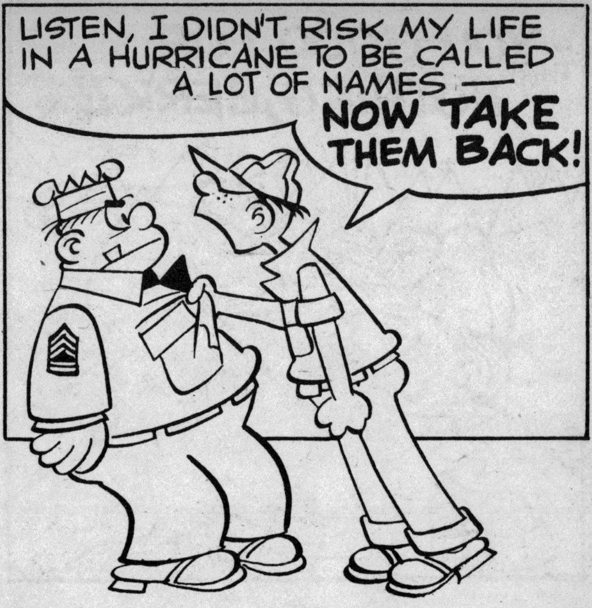
LISTEN, I DIDN'T RISK MY LIFE IN A HURRICANE TO BE CALLED A LOT OF NAMES —
NOW TAKE THEM BACK!

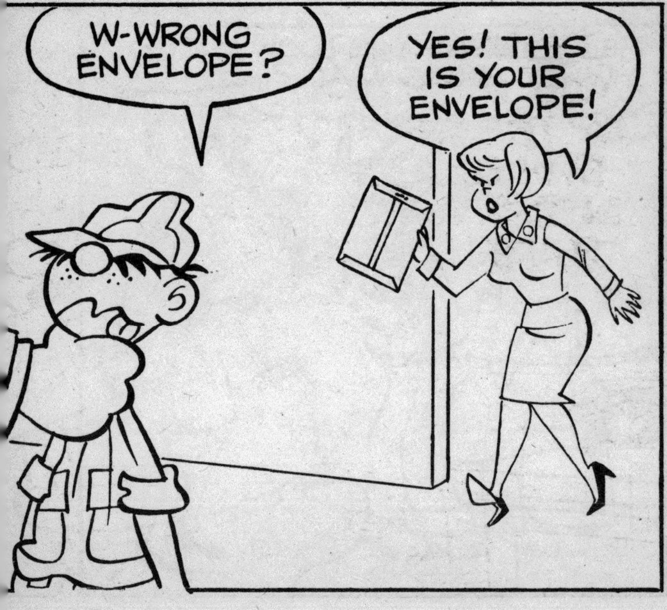
W-WRONG ENVELOPE?
YES! THIS IS YOUR ENVELOPE!

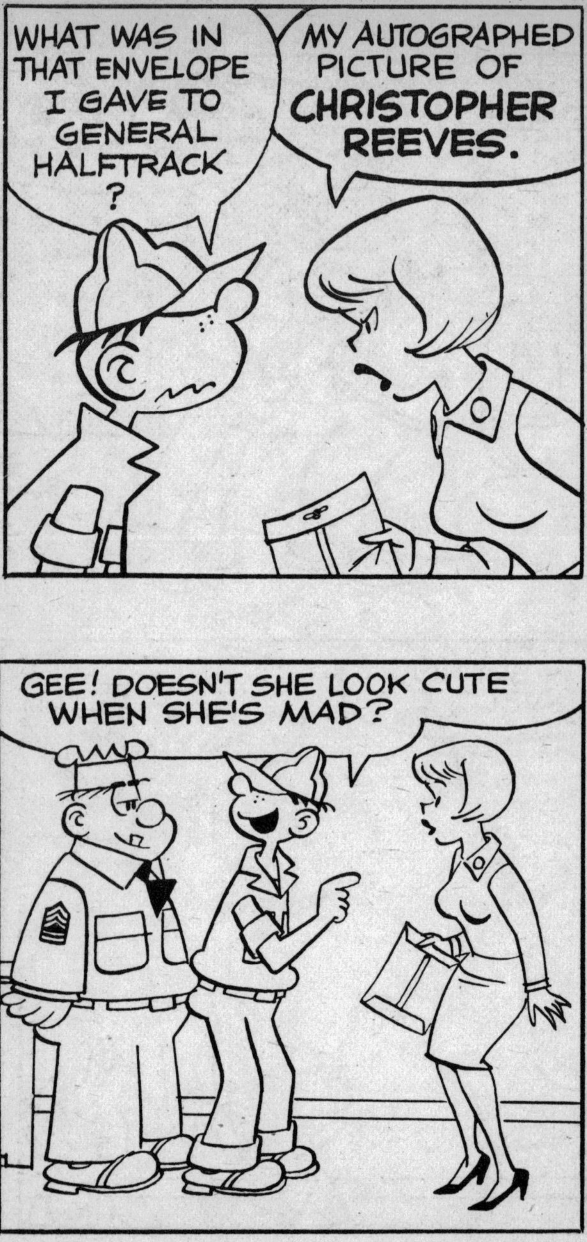
WHAT WAS IN THAT ENVELOPE I GAVE TO GENERAL HALFTRACK ?
MY AUTOGRAPHED PICTURE OF CHRISTOPHER REEVES.
GEE! DOESN'T SHE LOOK CUTE WHEN SHE'S MAD?

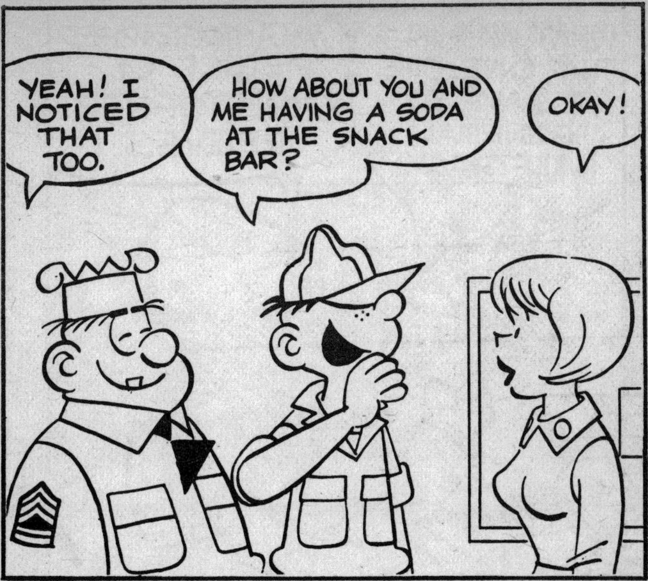
YEAH! I NOTICED THAT TOO.
HOW ABOUT YOU AND ME HAVING A SODA AT THE SNACK BAR?
OKAY!

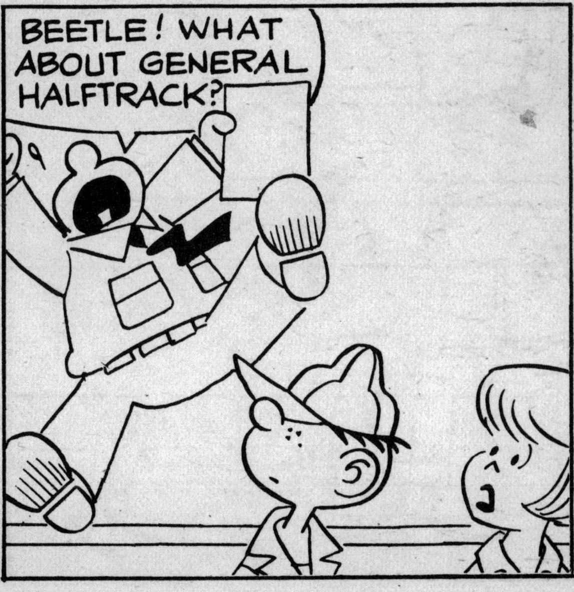
BEETLE! WHAT ABOUT GENERAL HALFTRACK?

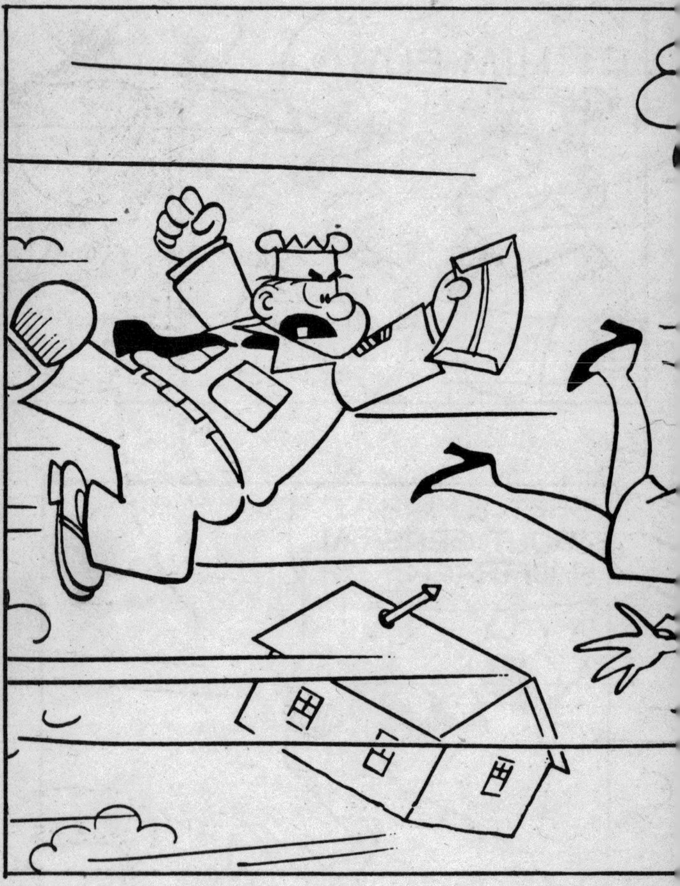

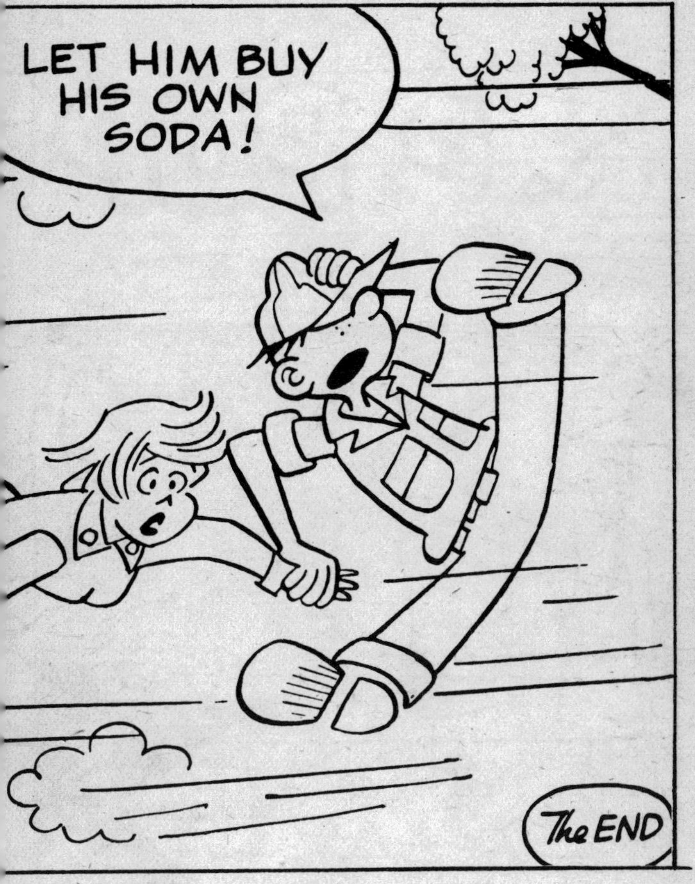
LET HIM BUY HIS OWN SODA!
The END

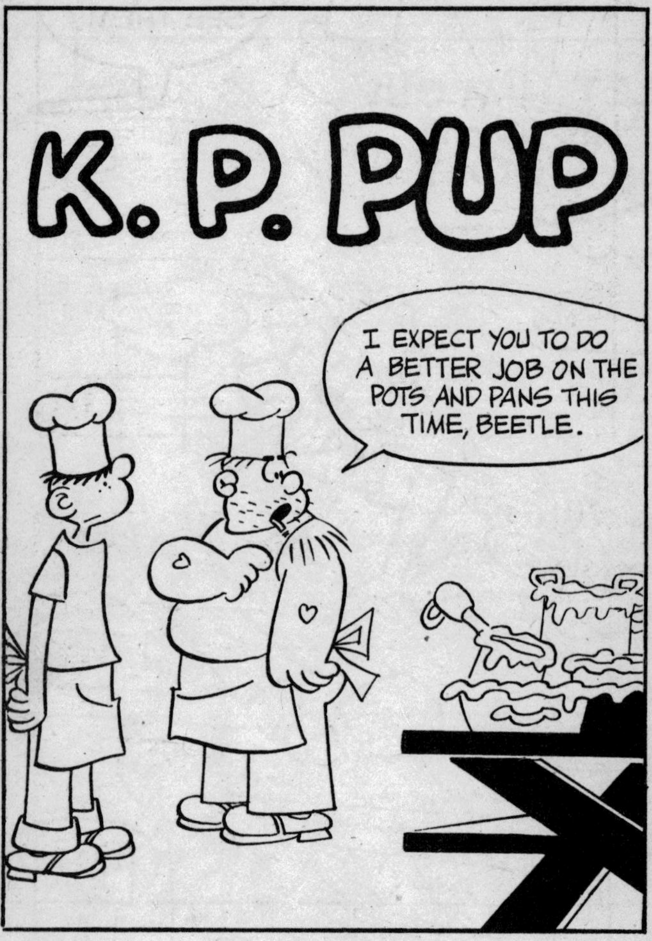
K. P. PUP
I EXPECT YOU TO DO A BETTER JOB ON THE POTS AND PANS THIS TIME, BEETLE.

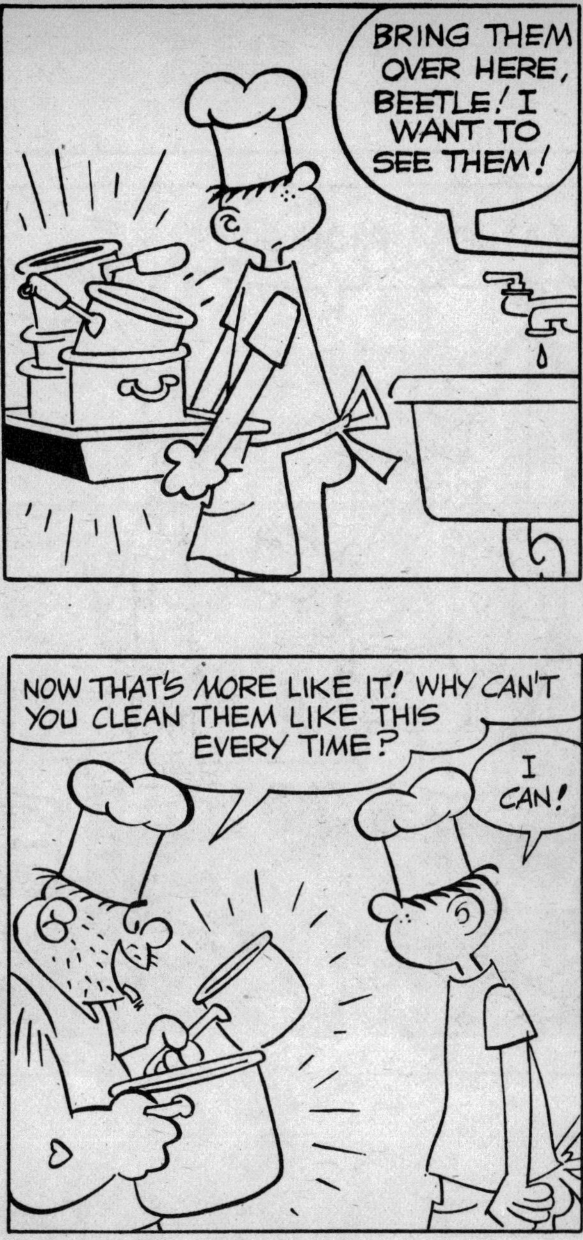
BRING THEM OVER HERE, BEETLE! I WANT TO SEE THEM!
NOW THAT'S MORE LIKE IT! WHY CAN'T YOU CLEAN THEM LIKE THIS EVERY TIME?
I CAN!

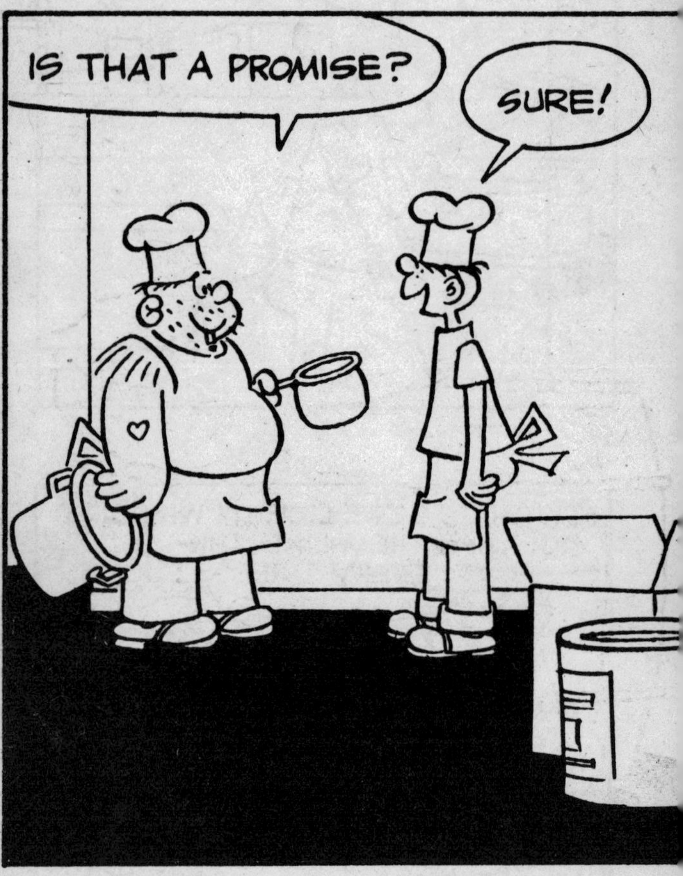
IS THAT A PROMISE?
SURE!

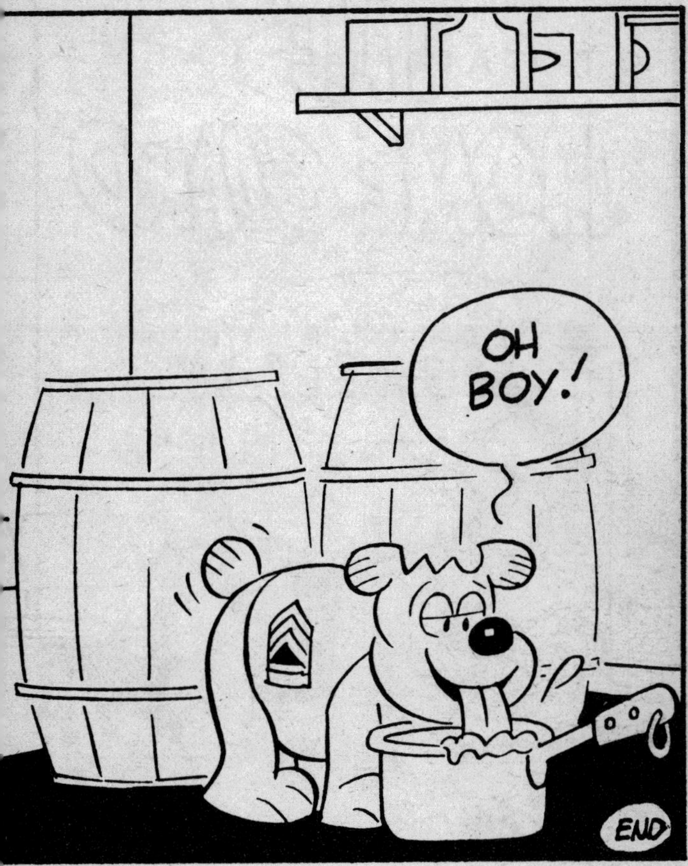
OH BOY!
END

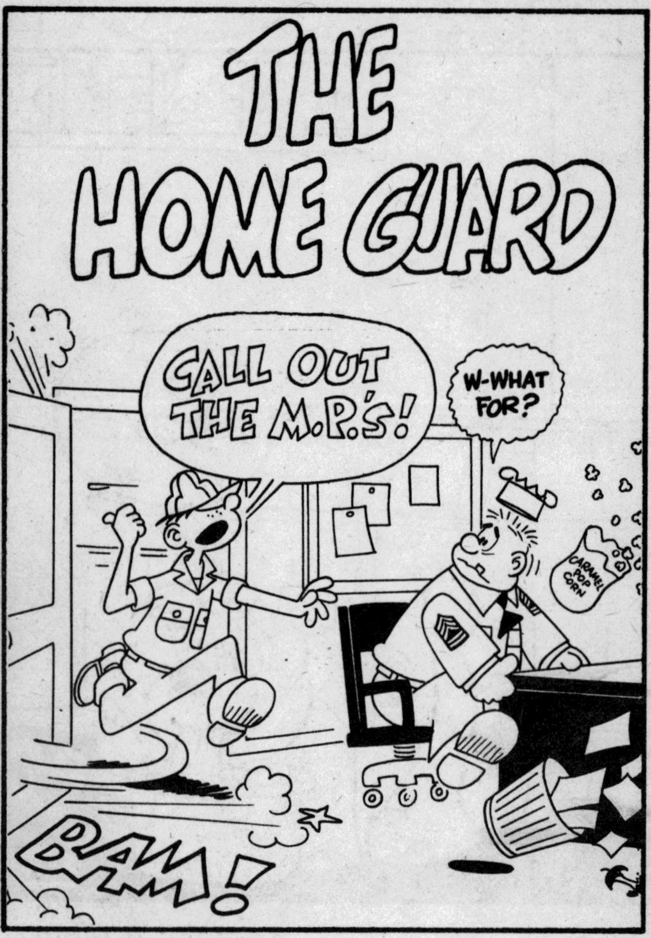
THE HOME GUARD
CALL OUT THE M.P.'s!
W-WHAT FOR?
CARAMEL POP CORN
BAM!

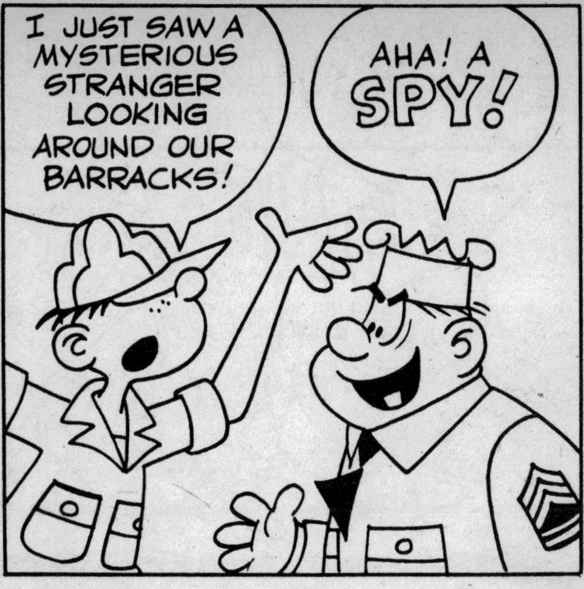
I JUST SAW A MYSTERIOUS STRANGER LOOKING AROUND OUR BARRACKS!
AHA! A SPY!

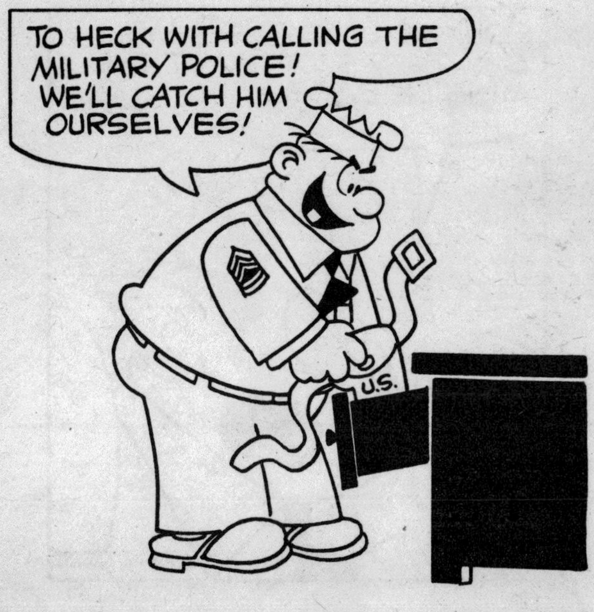
TO HECK WITH CALLING THE MILITARY POLICE! WE'LL CATCH HIM OURSELVES!
U.S.

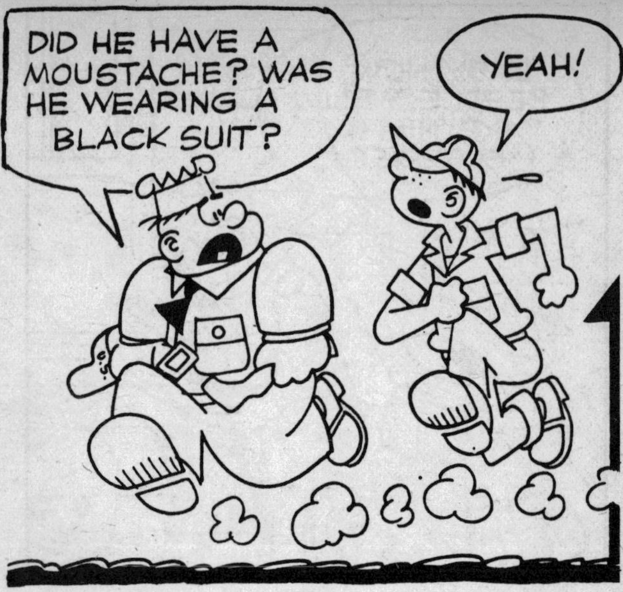
DID HE HAVE A MOUSTACHE? WAS HE WEARING A BLACK SUIT?
YEAH!

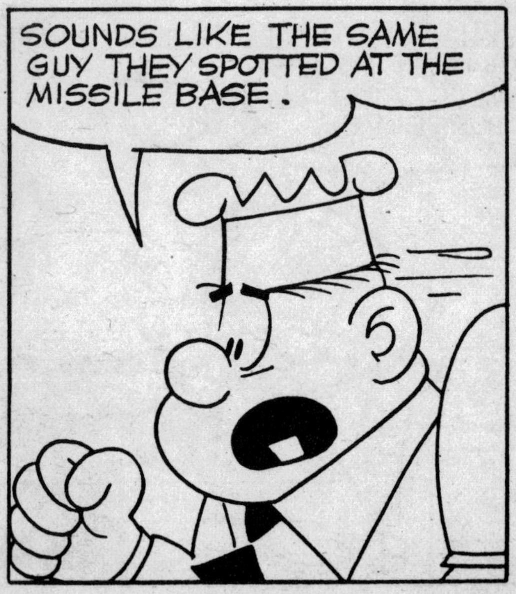
SOUNDS LIKE THE SAME GUY THEY SPOTTED AT THE MISSILE BASE.

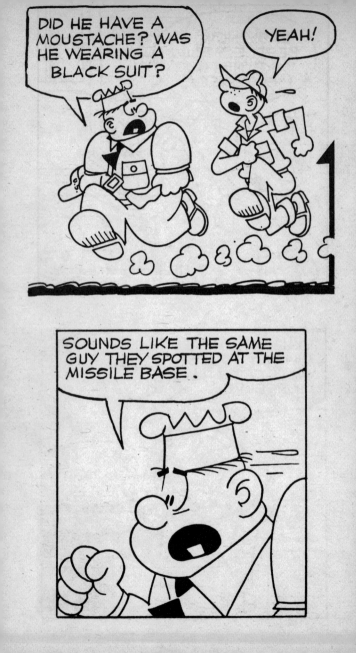

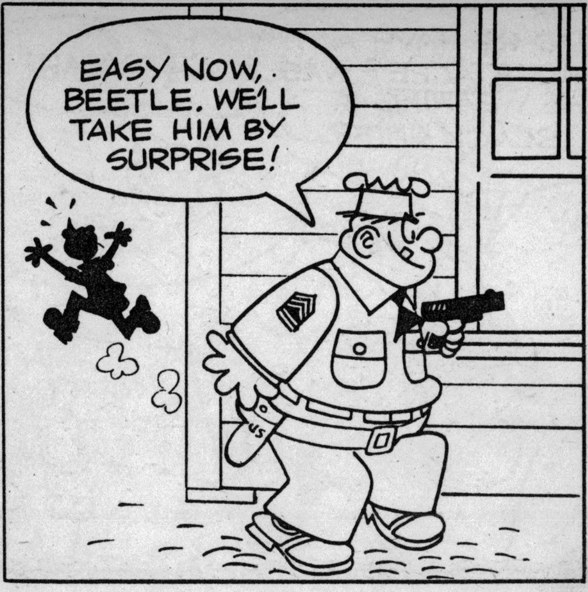
EASY NOW, BEETLE. WE'LL TAKE HIM BY SURPRISE!
US

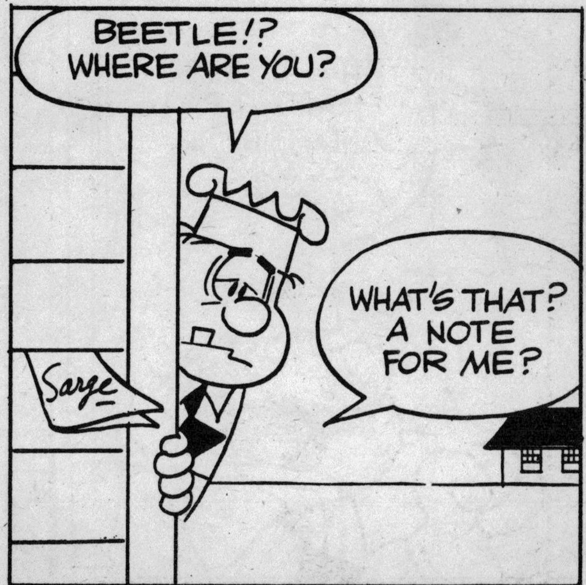
BEETLE!? WHERE ARE YOU?
WHAT'S THAT? A NOTE FOR ME?
Sarge

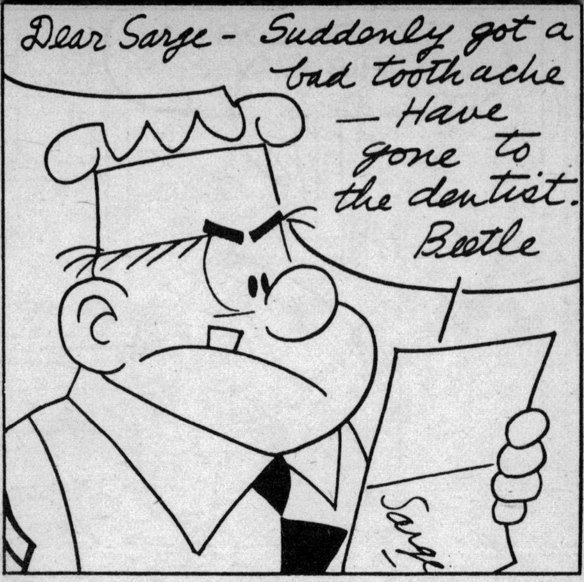
Dear Sarge - Suddenly got a bad toothache — Have gone to the dentist. Beetle
Sarge

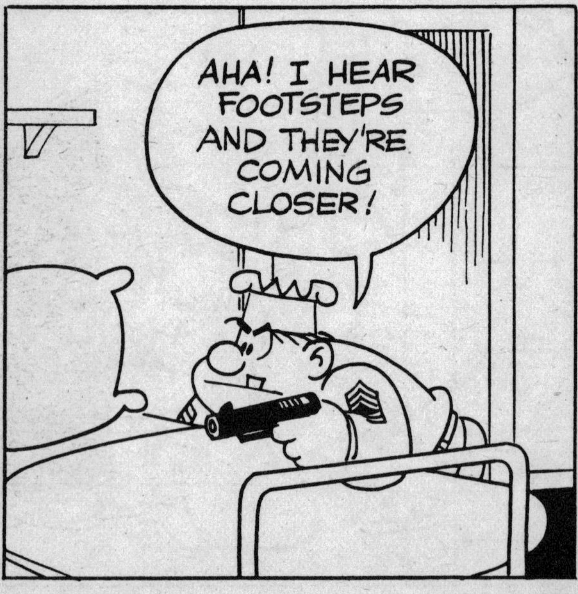
AHA! I HEAR FOOTSTEPS AND THEY'RE COMING CLOSER!

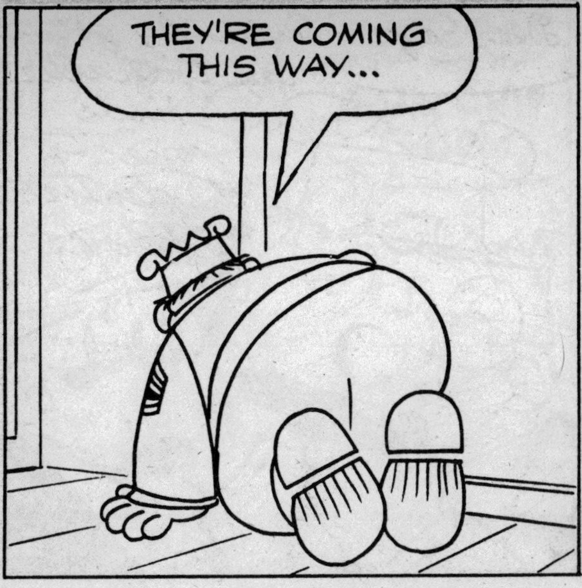
THEY'RE COMING THIS WAY...

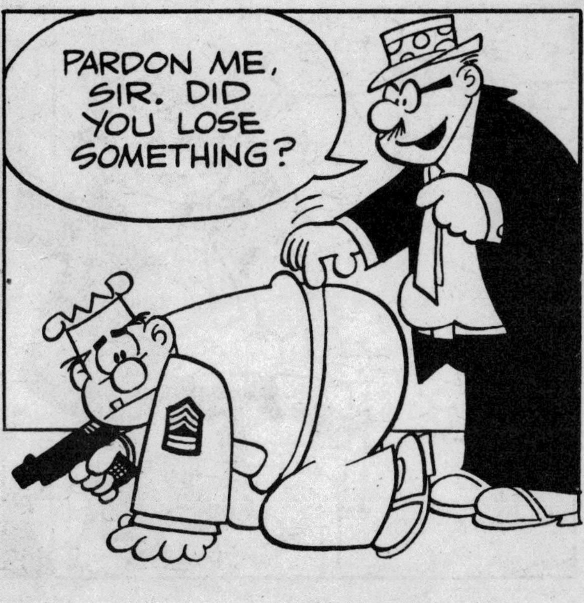
PARDON ME, SIR. DID YOU LOSE SOMETHING?

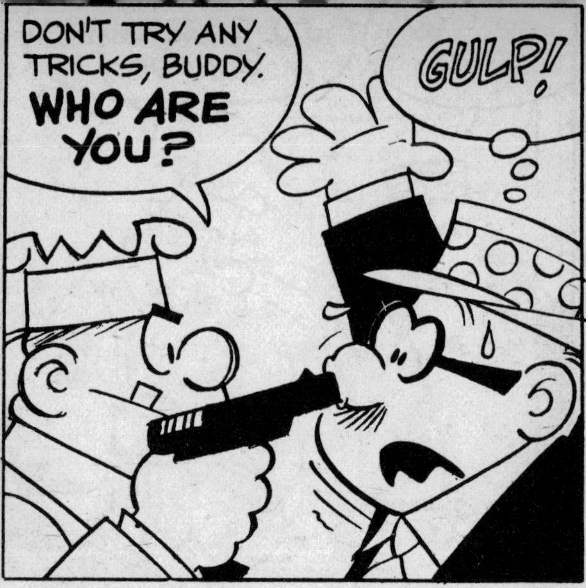
DON'T TRY ANY TRICKS, BUDDY. **WHO ARE YOU?**
GULP!

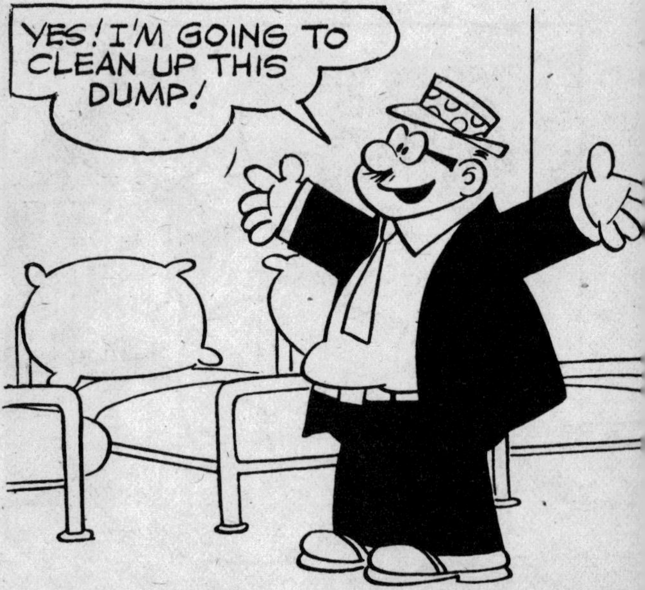
YES! I'M GOING TO CLEAN UP THIS DUMP!

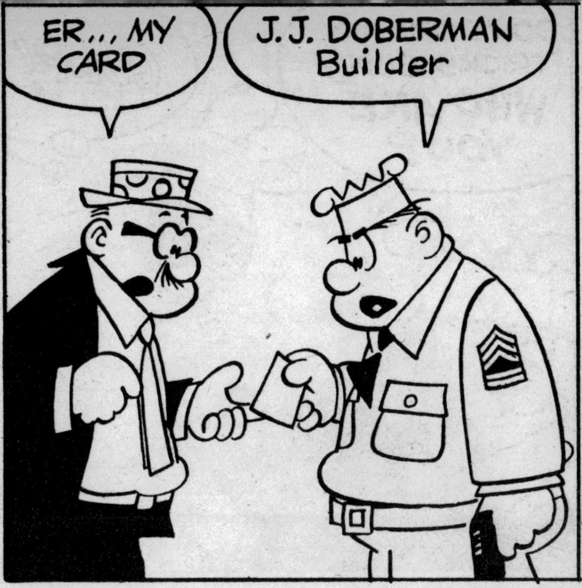
ER..., MY CARD
J. J. DOBERMAN Builder

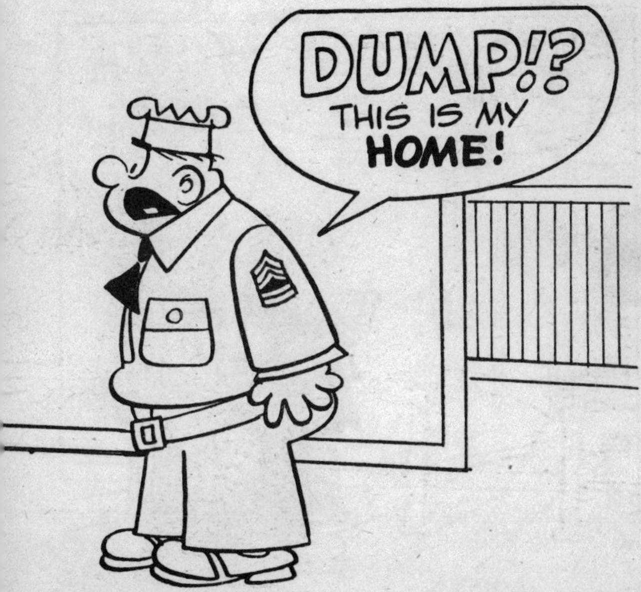
DUMP!? THIS IS MY HOME!

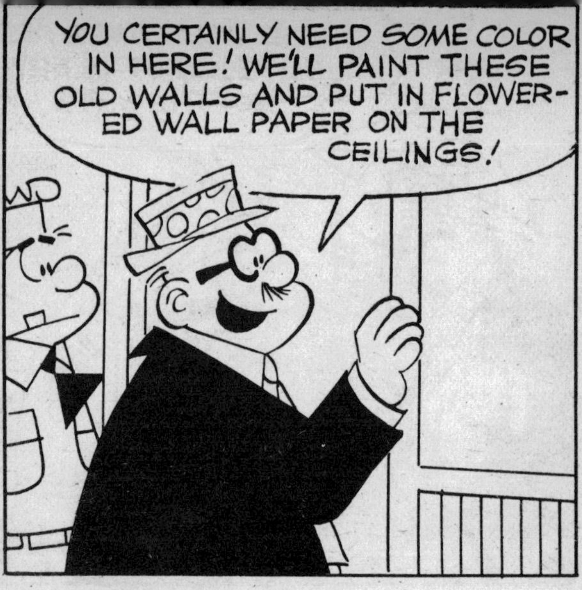
YOU CERTAINLY NEED SOME COLOR IN HERE! WE'LL PAINT THESE OLD WALLS AND PUT IN FLOWER-ED WALL PAPER ON THE CEILINGS!

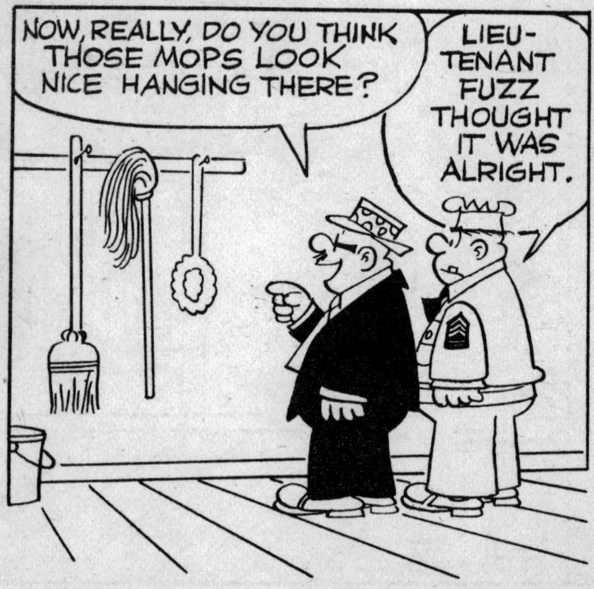
NOW, REALLY, DO YOU THINK THOSE MOPS LOOK NICE HANGING THERE?
LIEU-TENANT FUZZ THOUGHT IT WAS ALRIGHT.

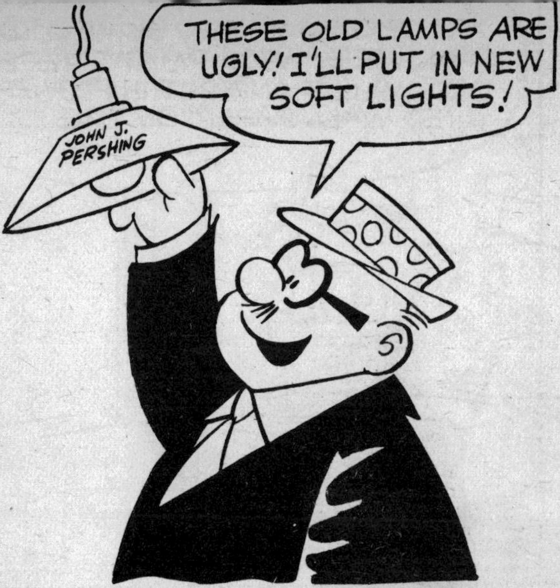
THESE OLD LAMPS ARE UGLY! I'LL PUT IN NEW SOFT LIGHTS!
JOHN J. PERSHING

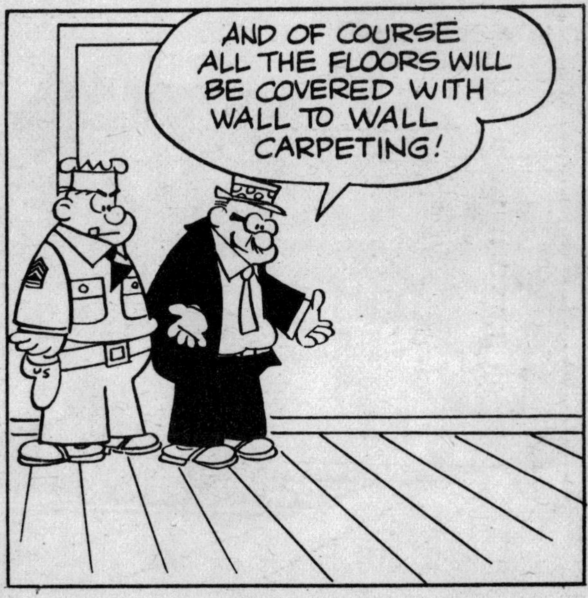
AND OF COURSE ALL THE FLOORS WILL BE COVERED WITH WALL TO WALL CARPETING!
US

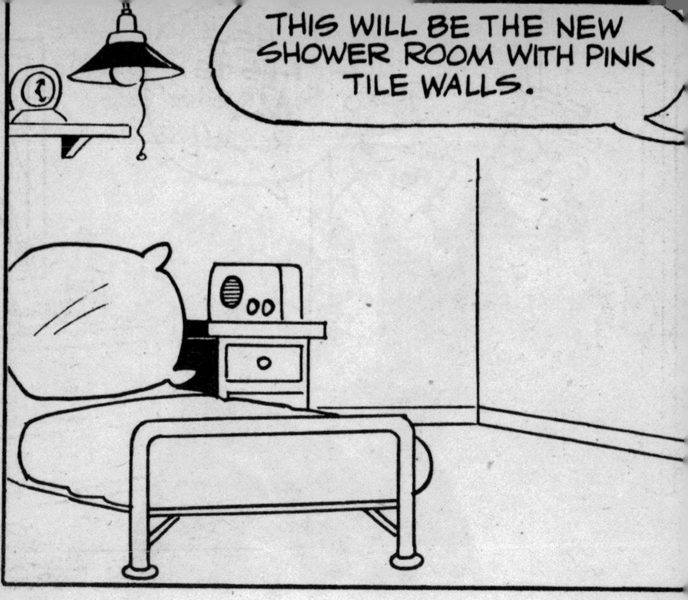
THIS WILL BE THE NEW SHOWER ROOM WITH PINK TILE WALLS.

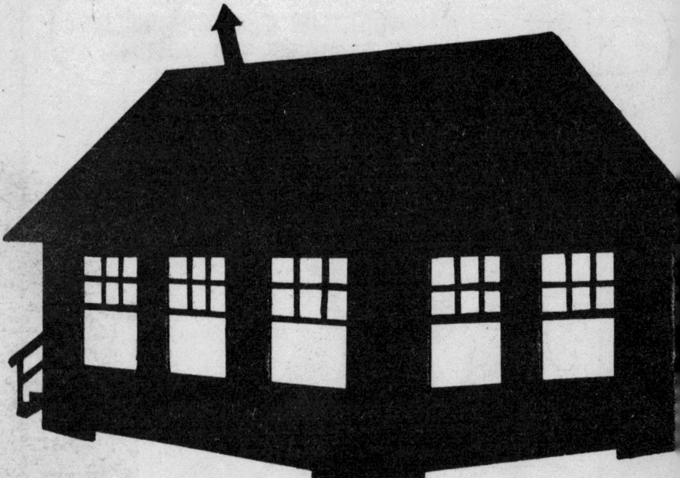

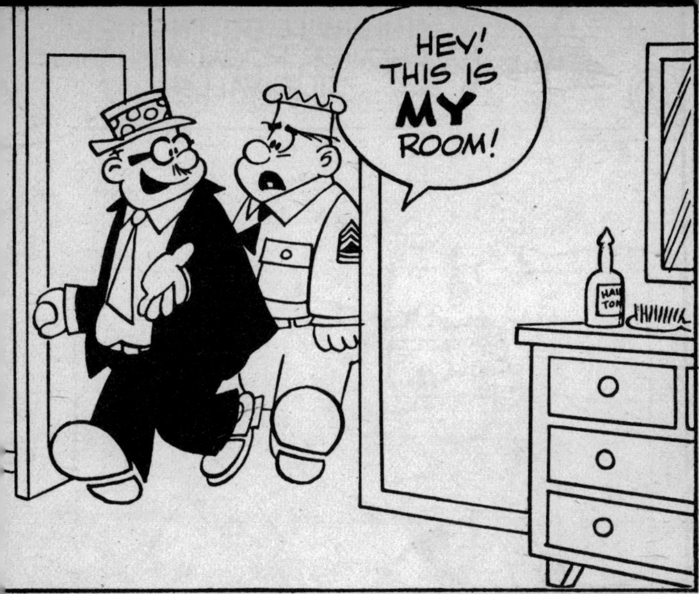
HEY! THIS IS MY ROOM!

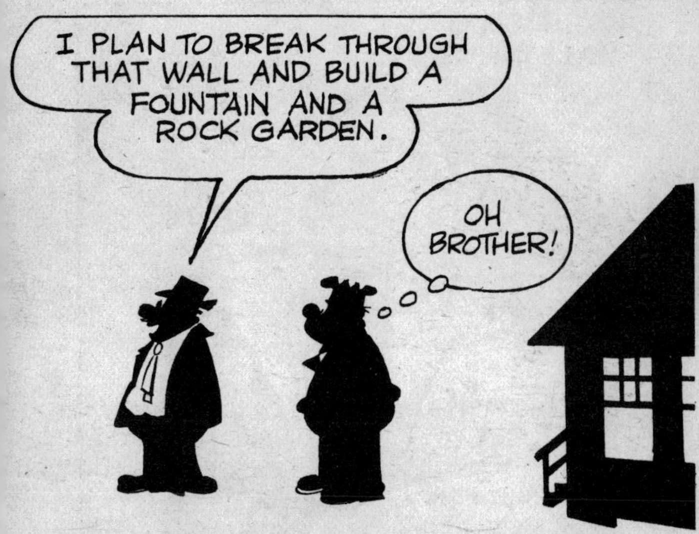
I PLAN TO BREAK THROUGH THAT WALL AND BUILD A FOUNTAIN AND A ROCK GARDEN.
OH BROTHER!

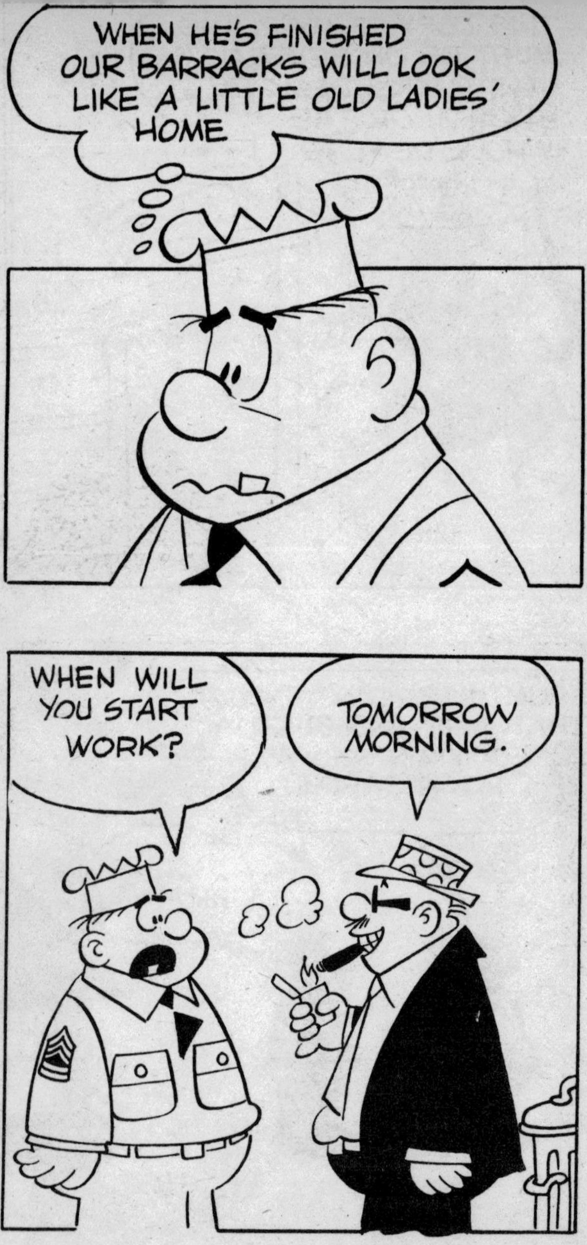
WHEN HE'S FINISHED OUR BARRACKS WILL LOOK LIKE A LITTLE OLD LADIES' HOME
WHEN WILL YOU START WORK?
TOMORROW MORNING.

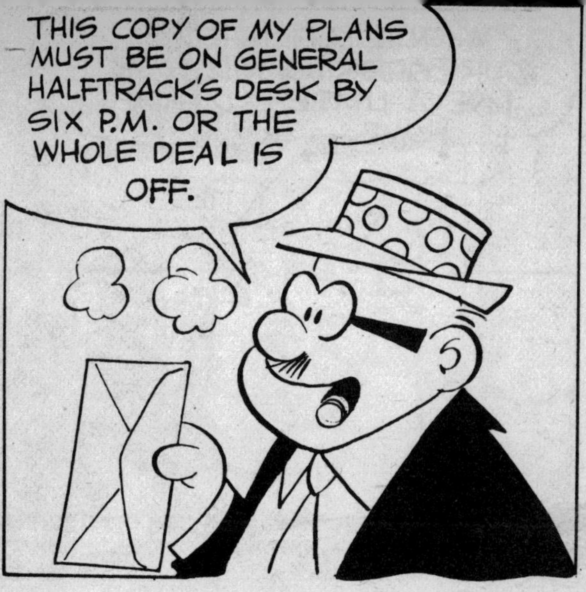
THIS COPY OF MY PLANS MUST BE ON GENERAL HALFTRACK'S DESK BY SIX P.M. OR THE WHOLE DEAL IS OFF.

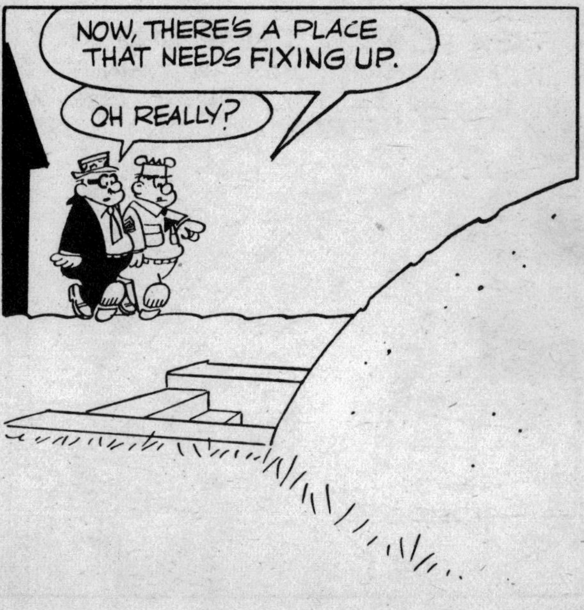
NOW, THERE'S A PLACE THAT NEEDS FIXING UP.
OH REALLY?

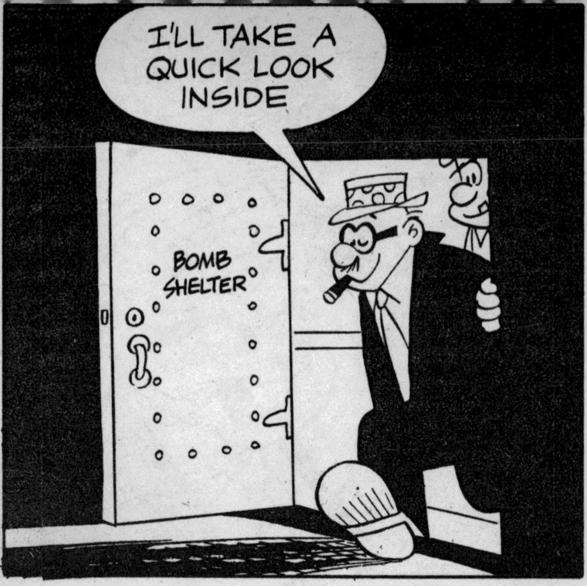
I'LL TAKE A QUICK LOOK INSIDE
BOMB SHELTER

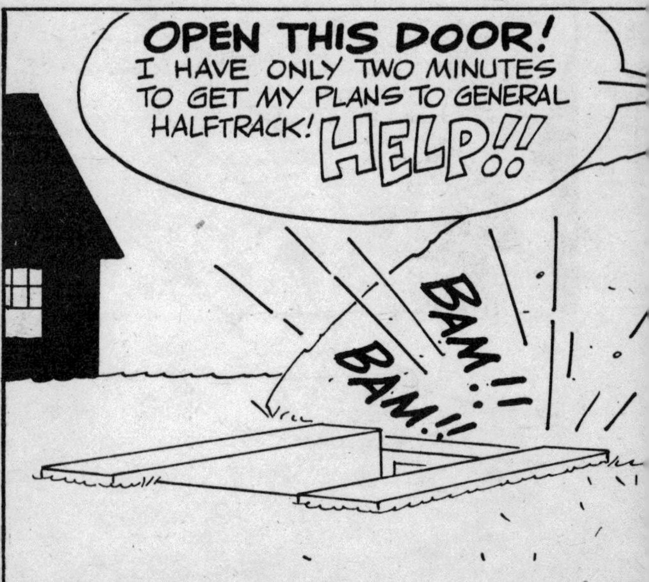
OPEN THIS DOOR! I HAVE ONLY TWO MINUTES TO GET MY PLANS TO GENERAL HALFTRACK! HELP!!
BAM!!
BAM!!

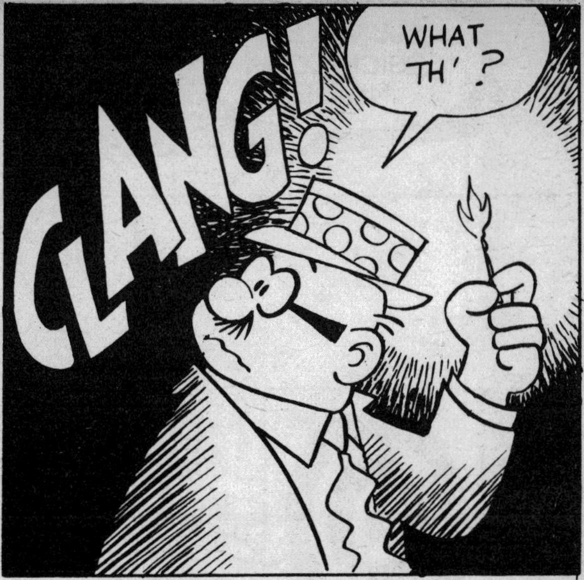
CLANG!
WHAT TH' ?

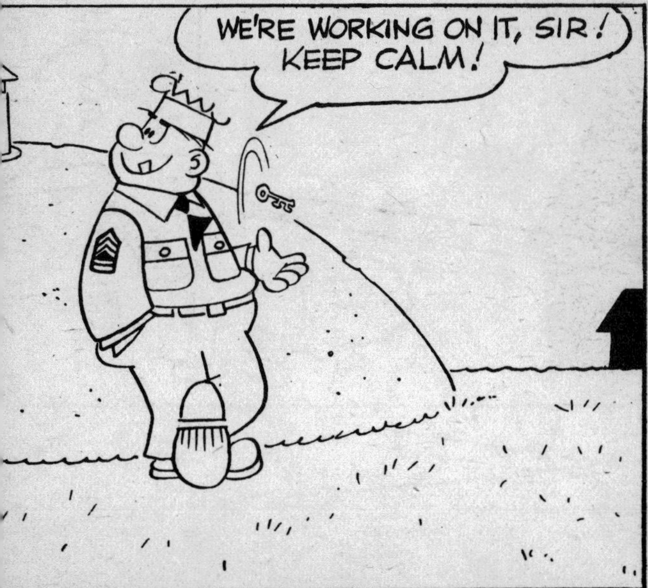
WE'RE WORKING ON IT, SIR! KEEP CALM!

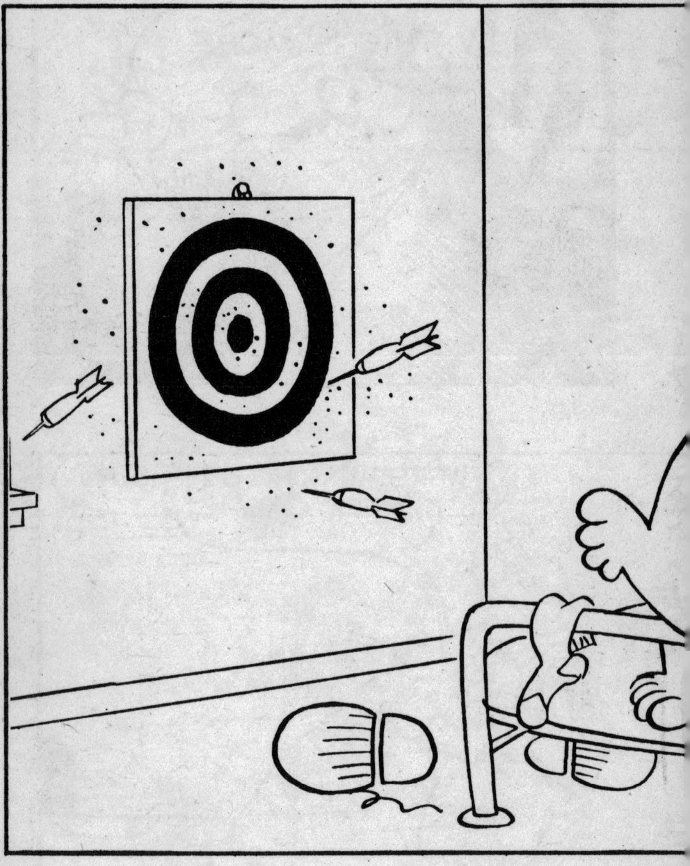

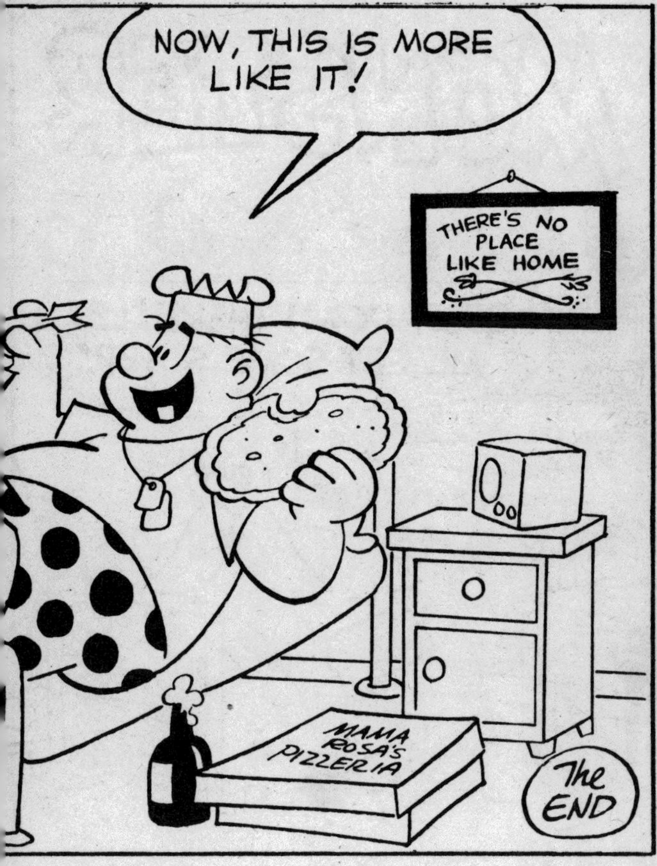
NOW, THIS IS MORE LIKE IT!
THERE'S NO PLACE LIKE HOME
MAMA ROSA'S PIZZERIA
The END

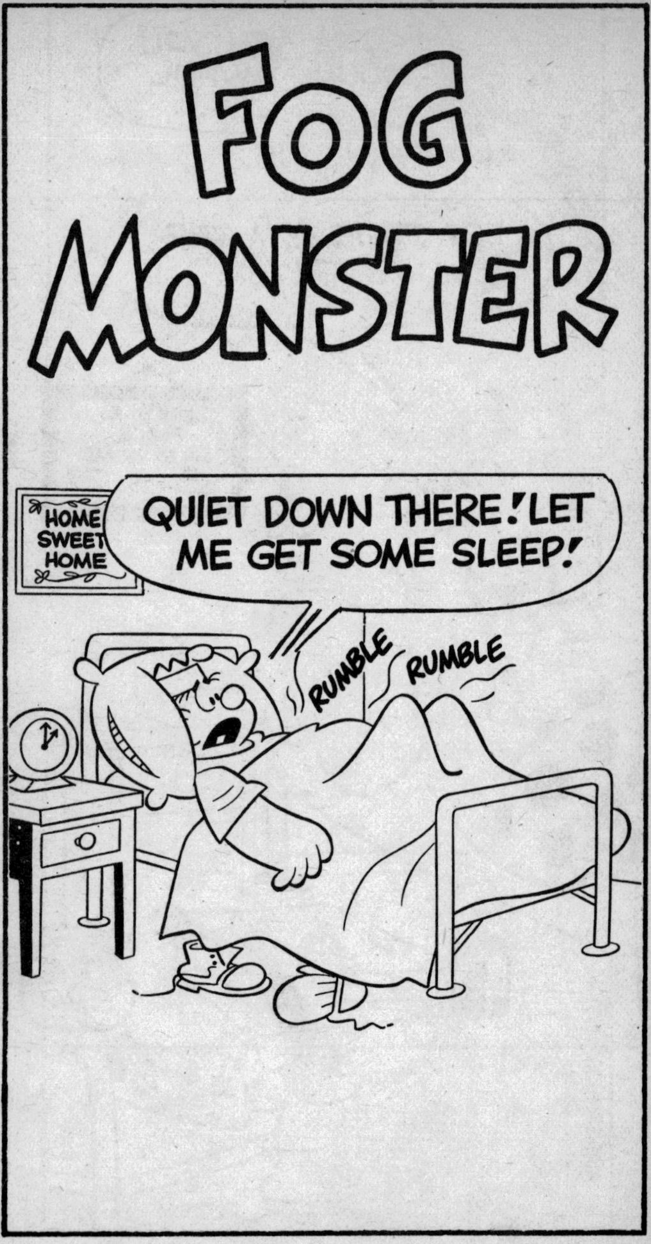
FOG MONSTER
HOME SWEET HOME
QUIET DOWN THERE! LET ME GET SOME SLEEP!
RUMBLE
RUMBLE

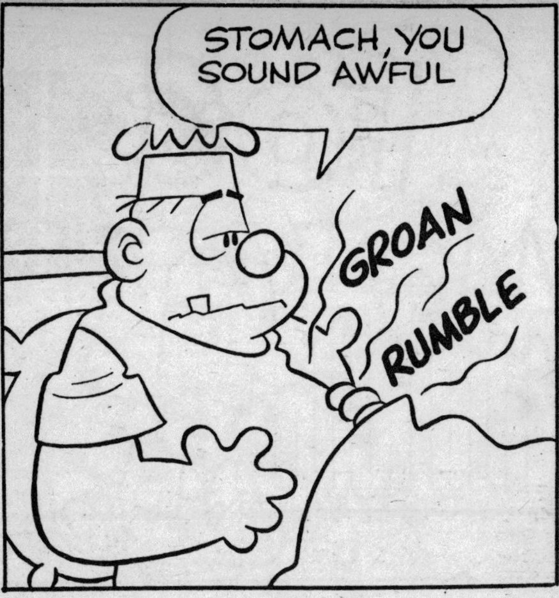
STOMACH, YOU SOUND AWFUL
GROAN
RUMBLE

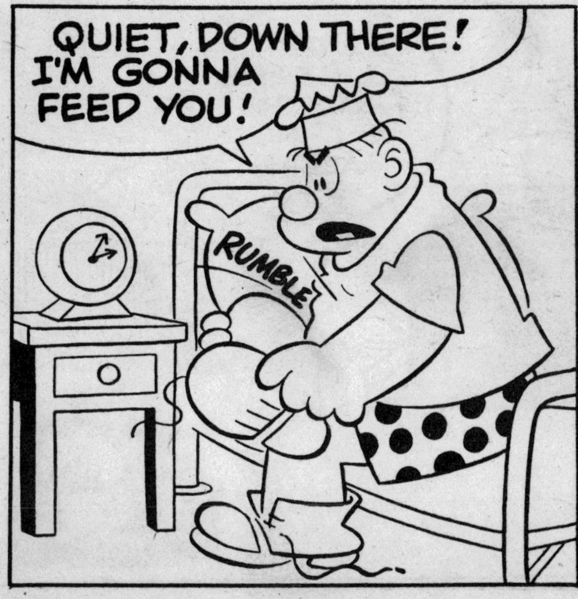
QUIET, DOWN THERE! I'M GONNA FEED YOU!
RUMBLE

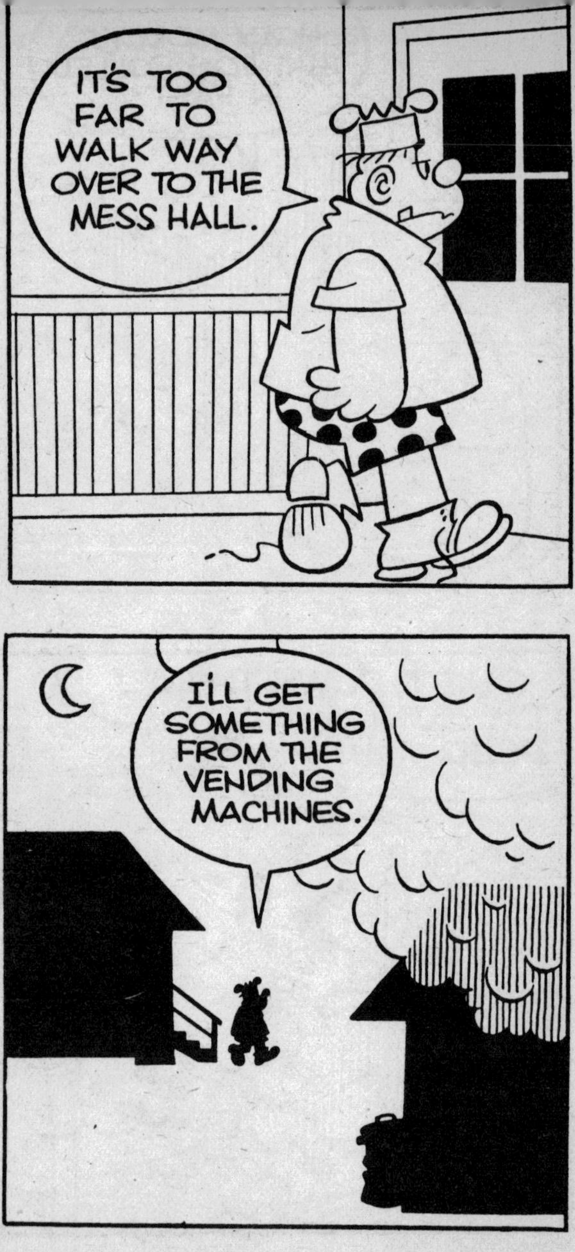
IT'S TOO FAR TO WALK WAY OVER TO THE MESS HALL.
I'LL GET SOMETHING FROM THE VENDING MACHINES.

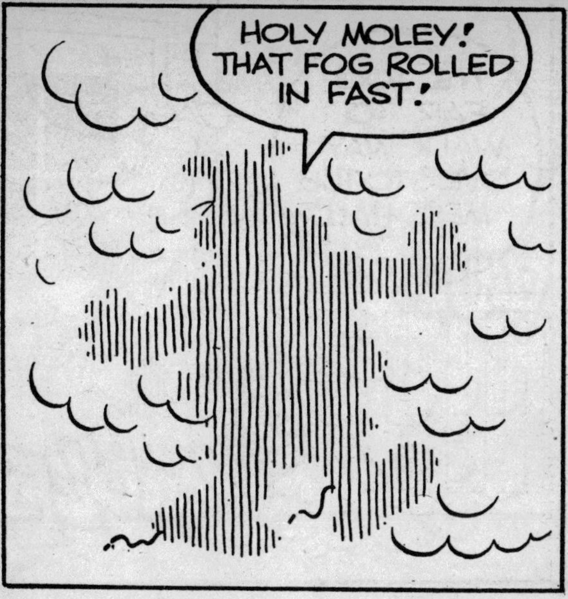
HOLY MOLEY! THAT FOG ROLLED IN FAST!

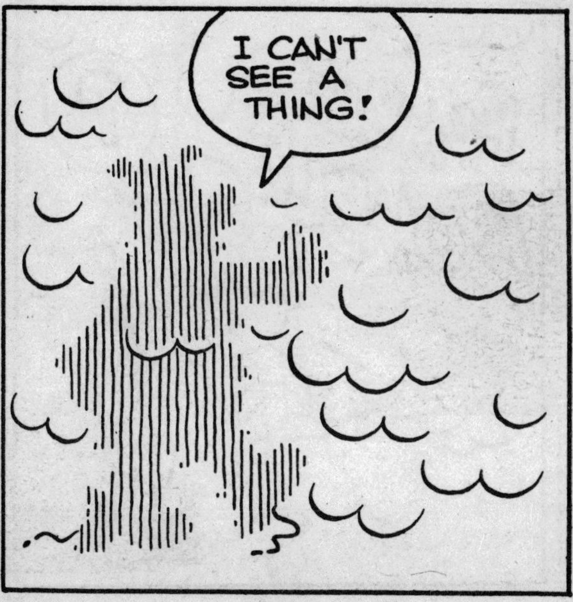
I CAN'T SEE A THING!

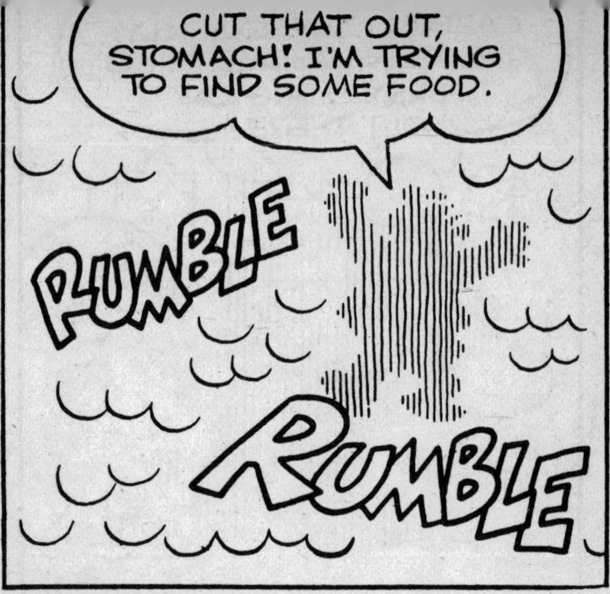
CUT THAT OUT, STOMACH! I'M TRYING TO FIND SOME FOOD.
RUMBLE
RUMBLE

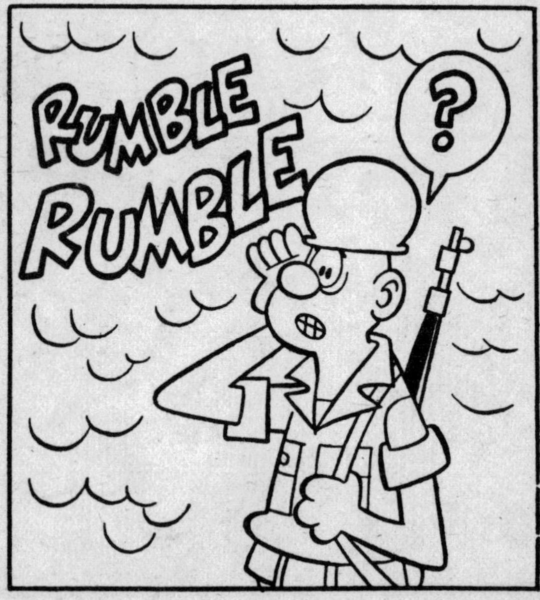
RUMBLE
RUMBLE
?

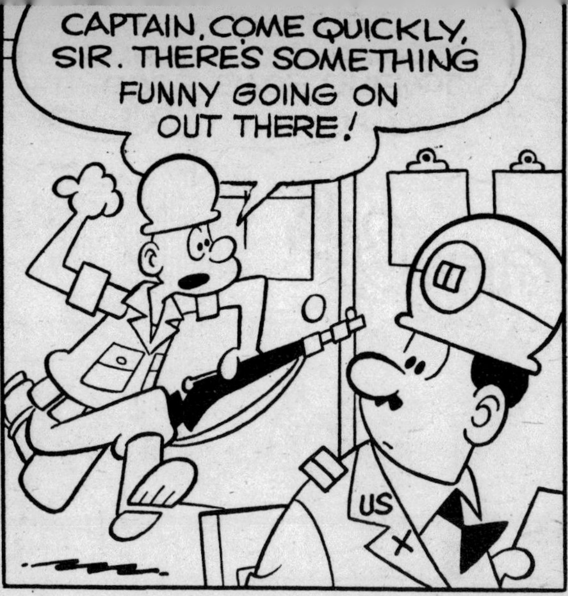
CAPTAIN, COME QUICKLY, SIR. THERE'S SOMETHING FUNNY GOING ON OUT THERE!
US

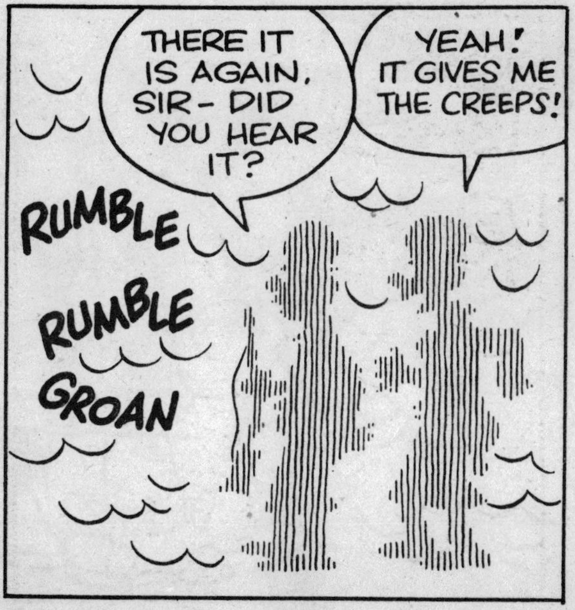
THERE IT IS AGAIN, SIR- DID YOU HEAR IT?
YEAH! IT GIVES ME THE CREEPS!
RUMBLE
RUMBLE
GROAN

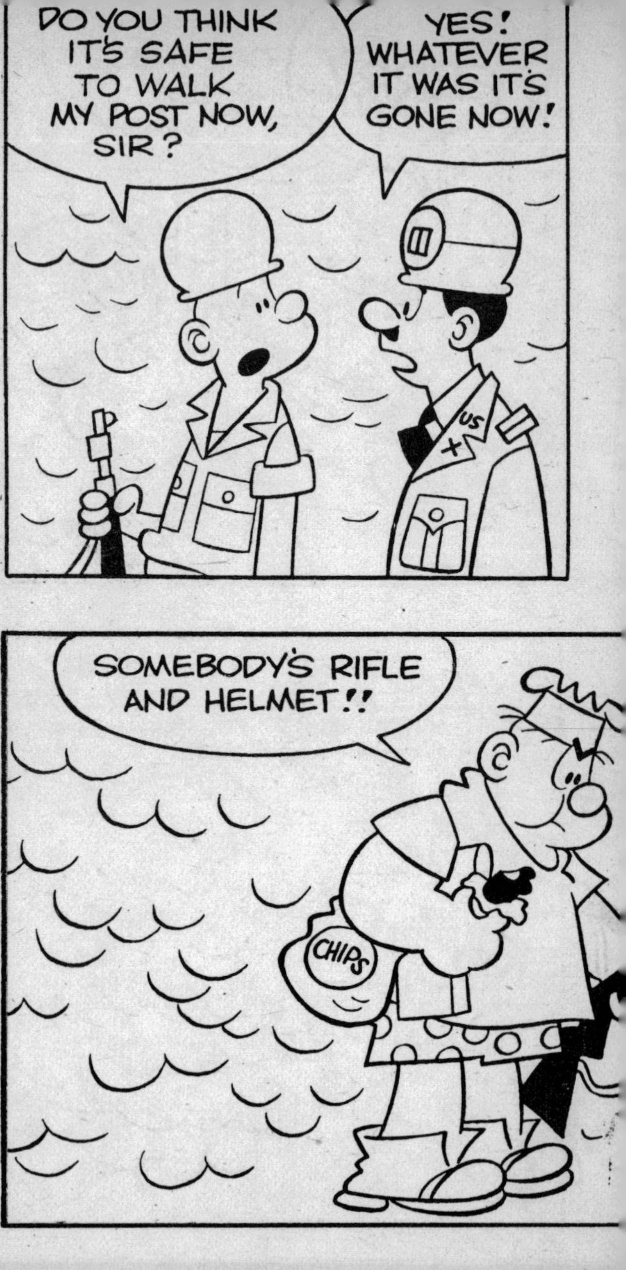
DO YOU THINK IT'S SAFE TO WALK MY POST NOW, SIR?
YES! WHATEVER IT WAS IT'S GONE NOW!
SOMEBODY'S RIFLE AND HELMET!!
CHIPS

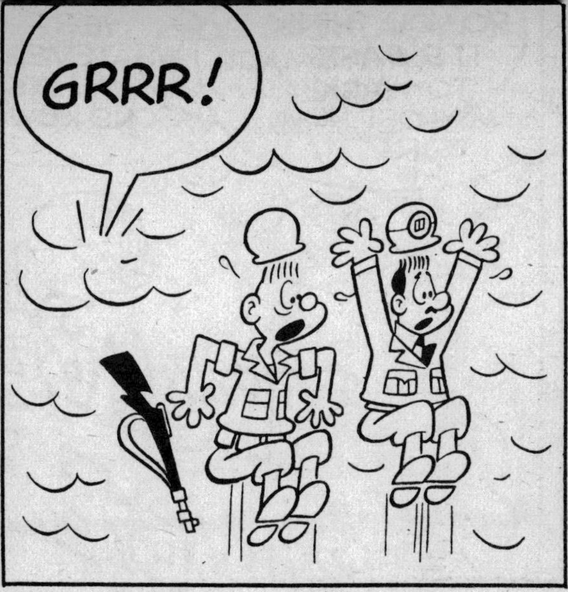
GRRR!

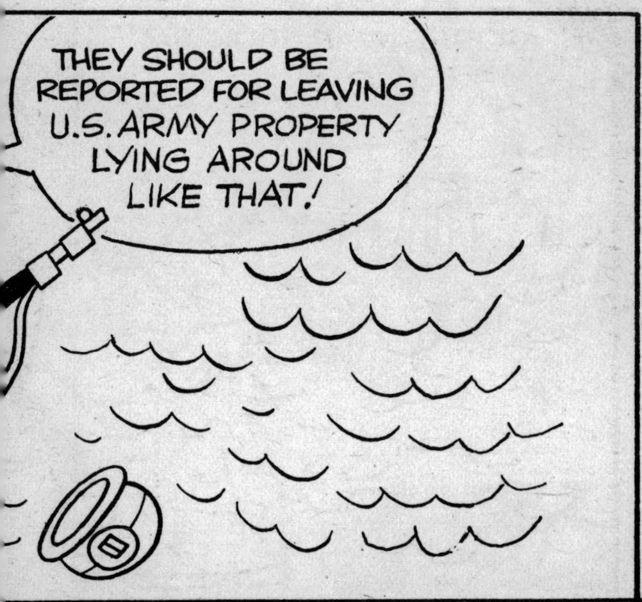
THEY SHOULD BE REPORTED FOR LEAVING U.S. ARMY PROPERTY LYING AROUND LIKE THAT!

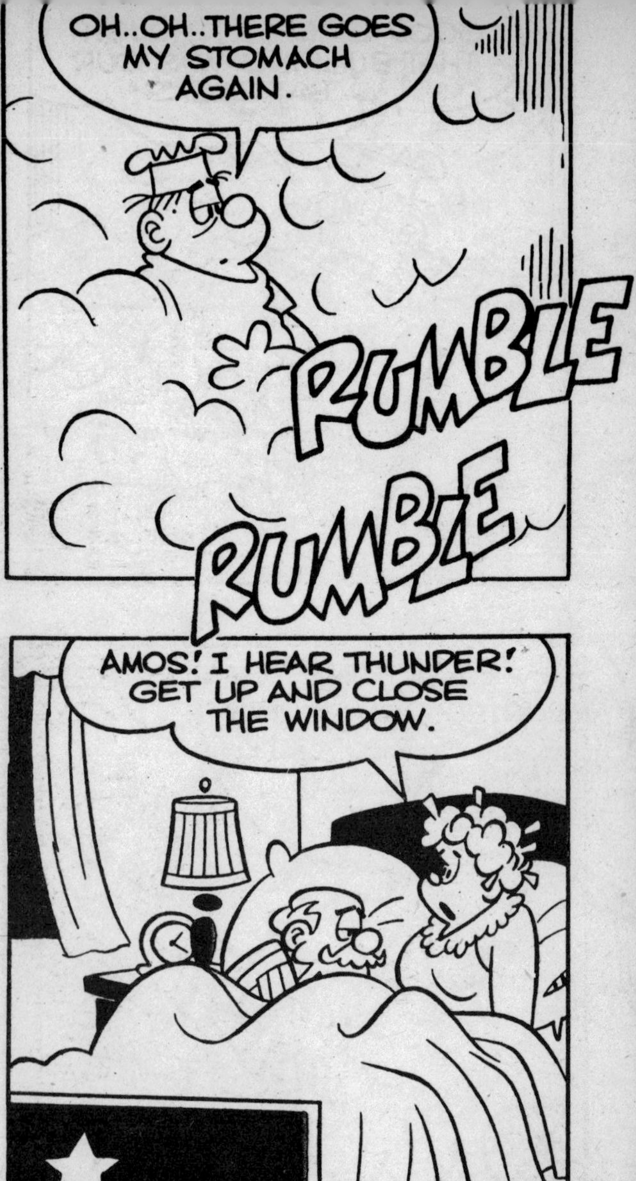
OH..OH..THERE GOES MY STOMACH AGAIN.
RUMBLE
RUMBLE
AMOS! I HEAR THUNDER! GET UP AND CLOSE THE WINDOW.

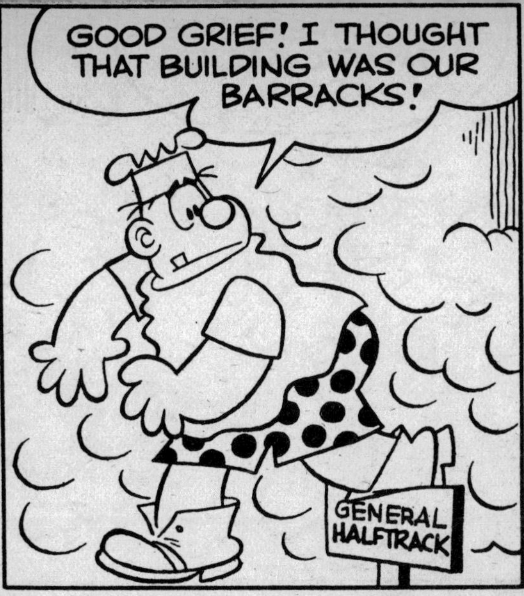
GOOD GRIEF! I THOUGHT THAT BUILDING WAS OUR BARRACKS!
GENERAL HALFTRACK

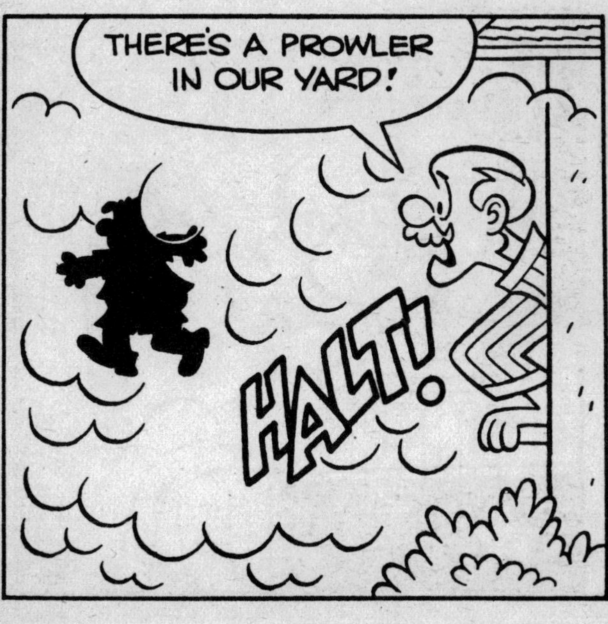
THERE'S A PROWLER IN OUR YARD!
HALT!

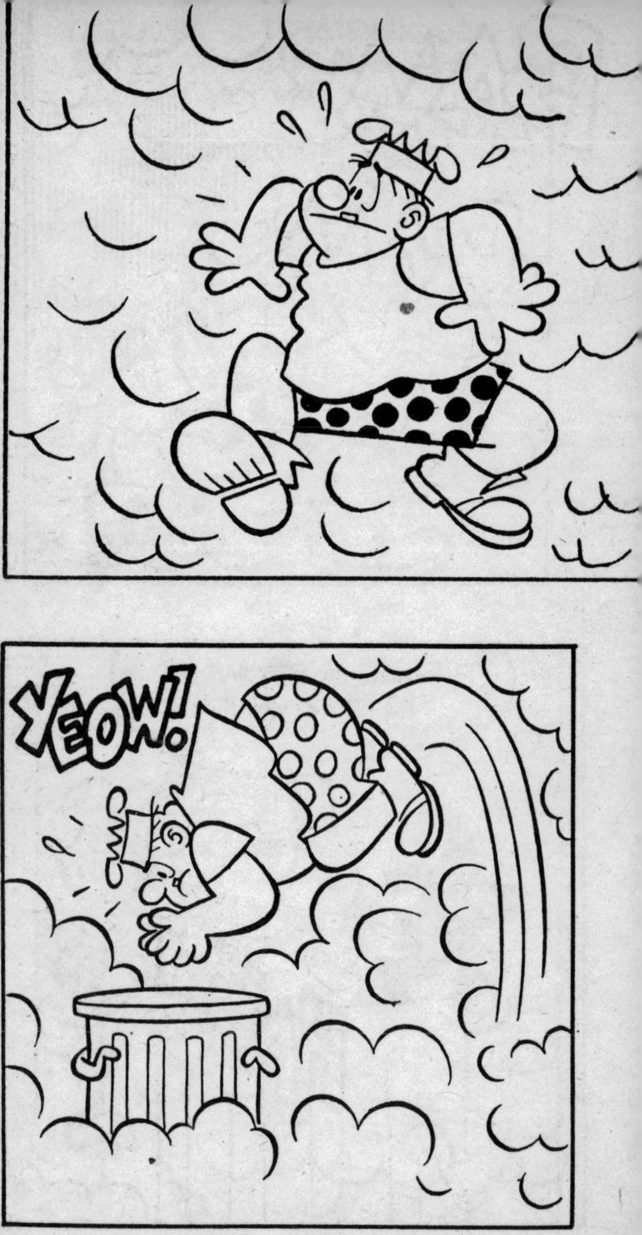
YEOW!

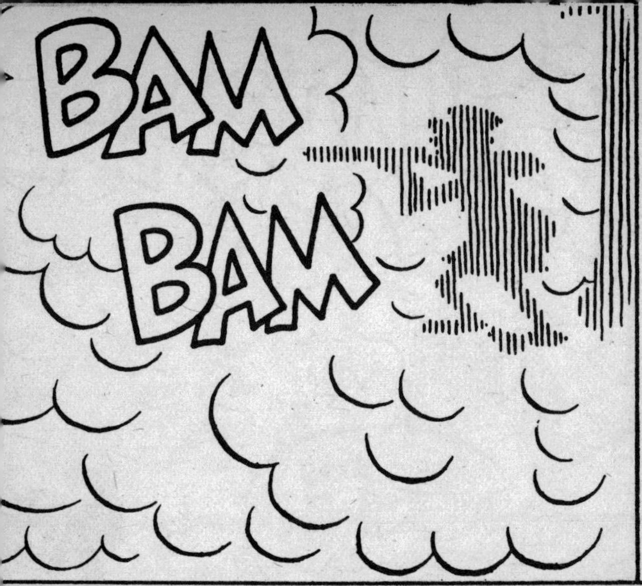
BAM
BAM

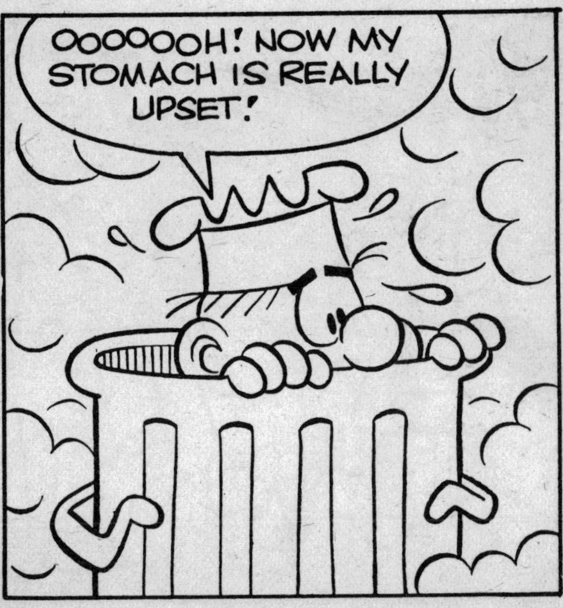
OOOOOOH! NOW MY STOMACH IS REALLY UPSET!

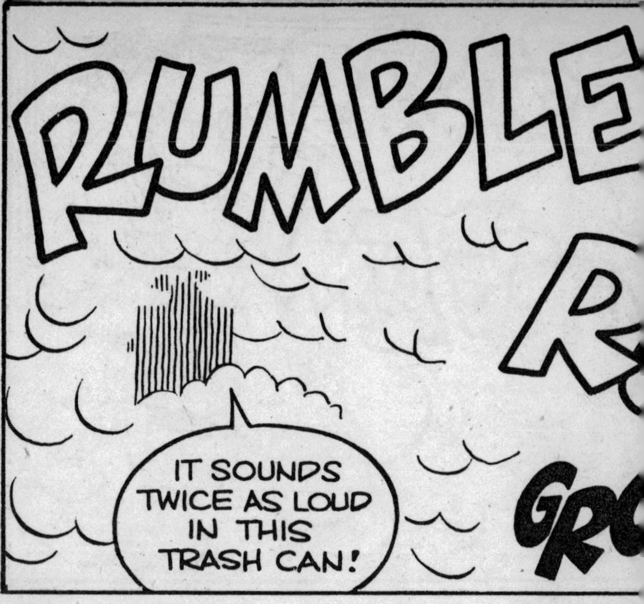
RUMBLE
R
GRO
IT SOUNDS TWICE AS LOUD IN THIS TRASH CAN!

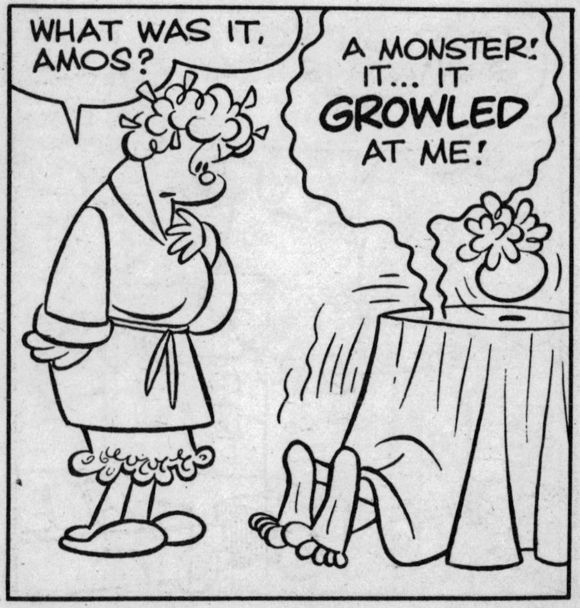
WHAT WAS IT, AMOS?
A MONSTER! IT... IT GROWLED AT ME!

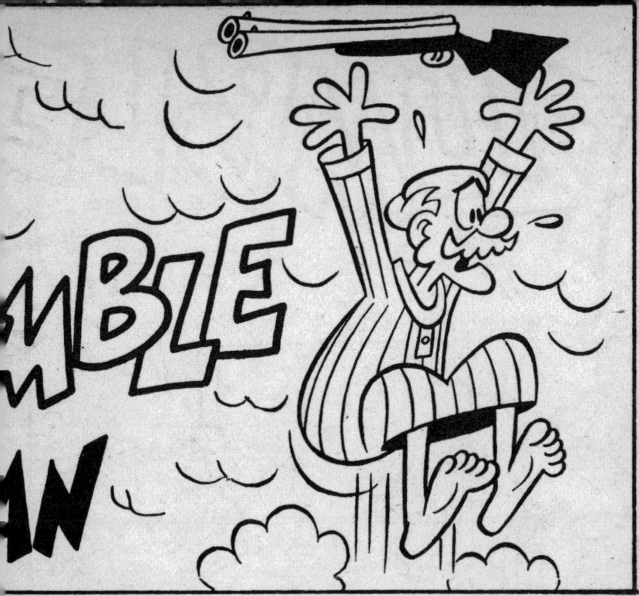

BLE
AN

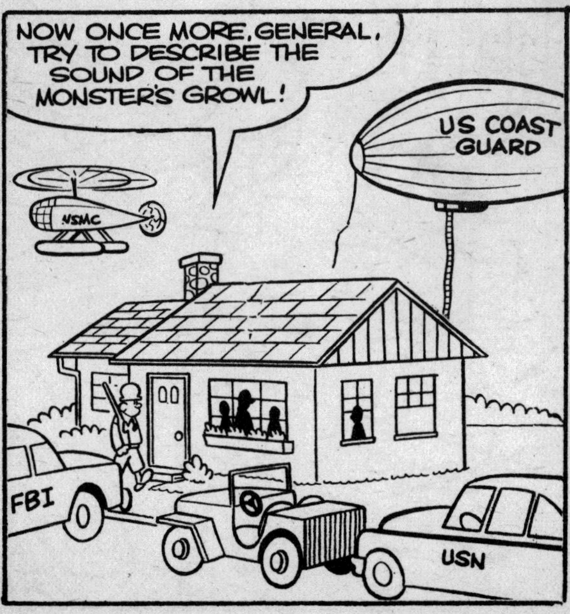

NOW ONCE MORE, GENERAL, TRY TO DESCRIBE THE SOUND OF THE MONSTER'S GROWL!
US COAST GUARD
USMC
FBI
USN

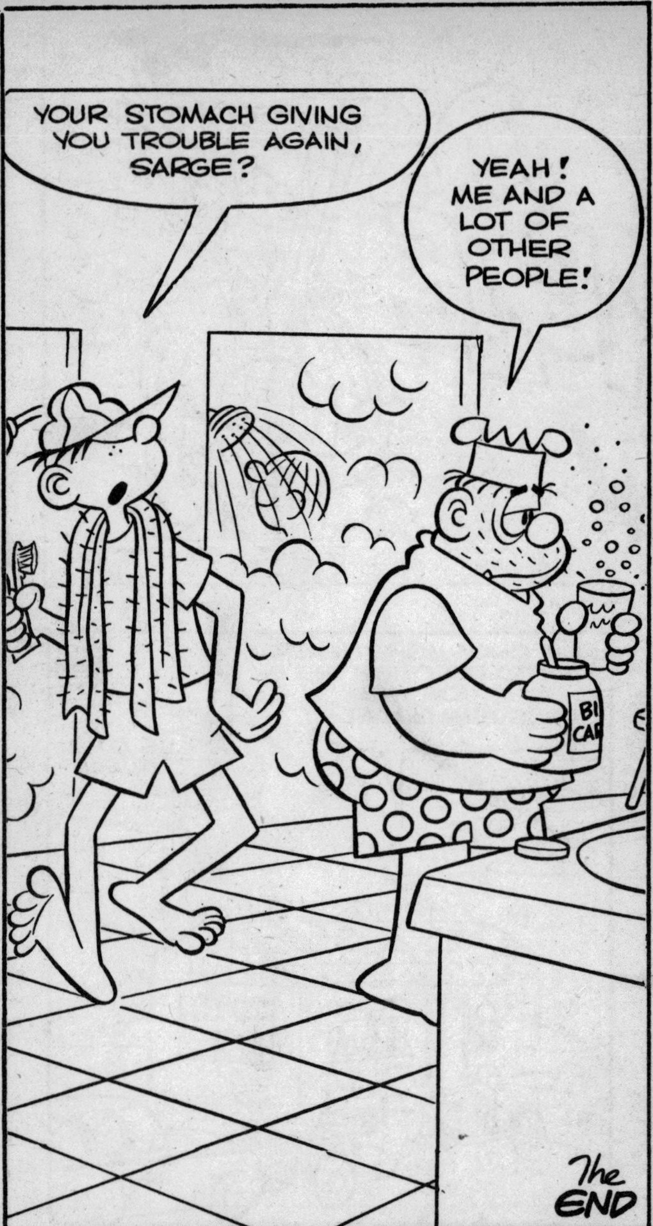
YOUR STOMACH GIVING YOU TROUBLE AGAIN, SARGE?
YEAH! ME AND A LOT OF OTHER PEOPLE!
BI CA
The END

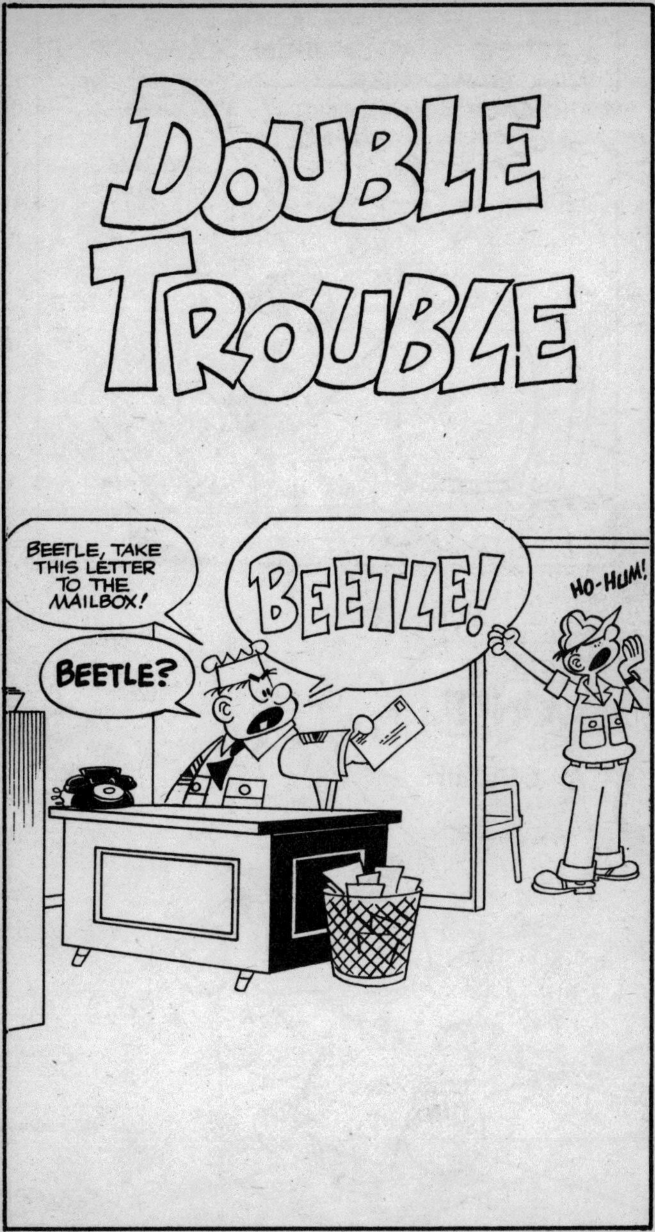
DOUBLE TROUBLE
BEETLE, TAKE THIS LETTER TO THE MAILBOX!
BEETLE?
BEETLE!
HO-HUM!

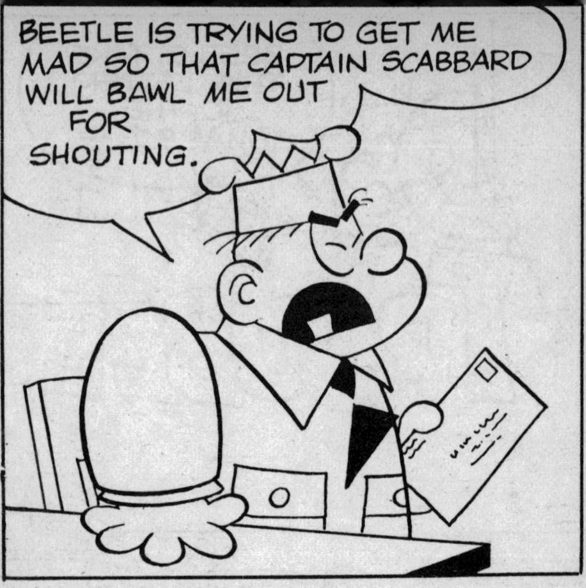
BEETLE IS TRYING TO GET ME MAD SO THAT CAPTAIN SCABBARD WILL BAWL ME OUT FOR SHOUTING.

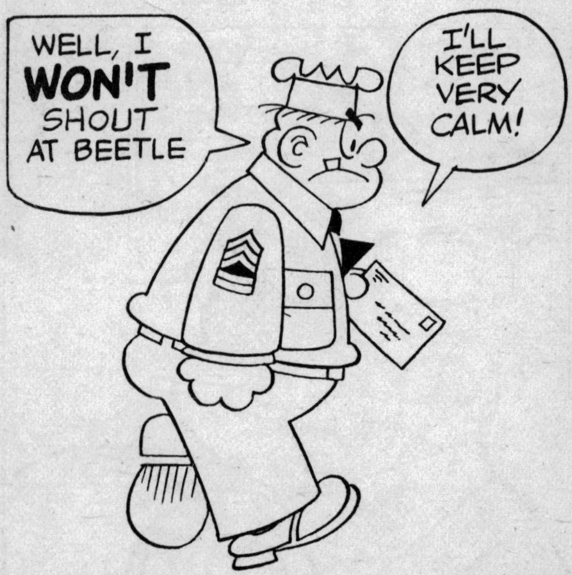
WELL, I **WON'T** SHOUT AT BEETLE
I'LL KEEP VERY CALM!

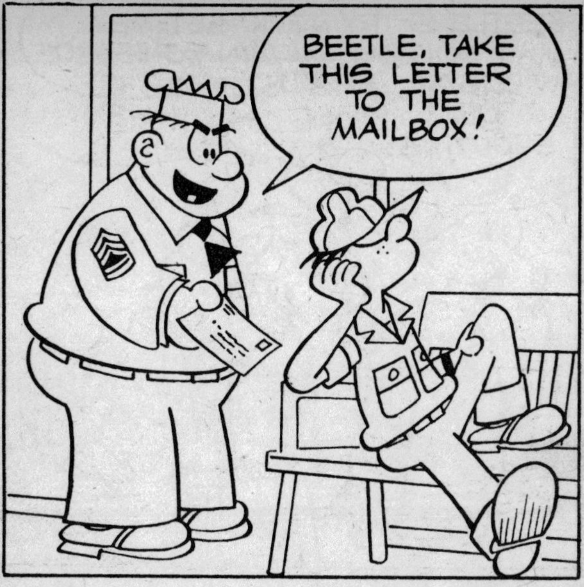
BEETLE, TAKE THIS LETTER TO THE MAILBOX!

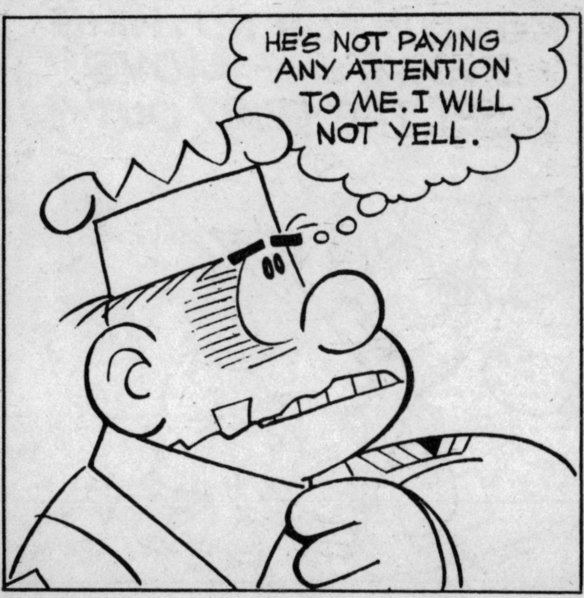
HE'S NOT PAYING ANY ATTENTION TO ME. I WILL NOT YELL.

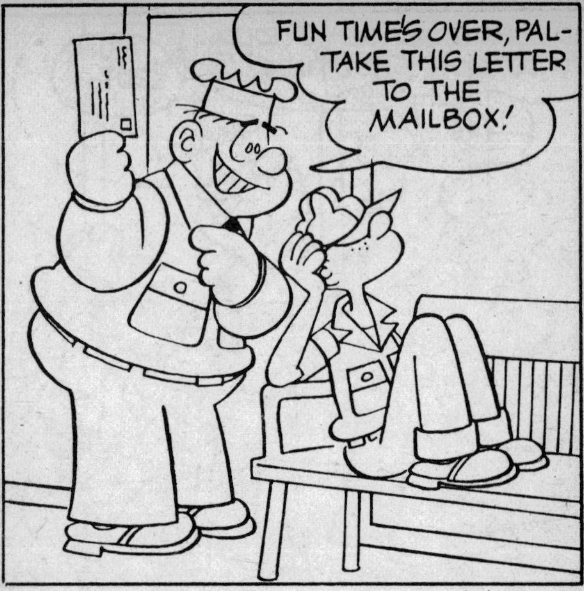
FUN TIME'S OVER, PAL-
TAKE THIS LETTER
TO THE
MAILBOX!

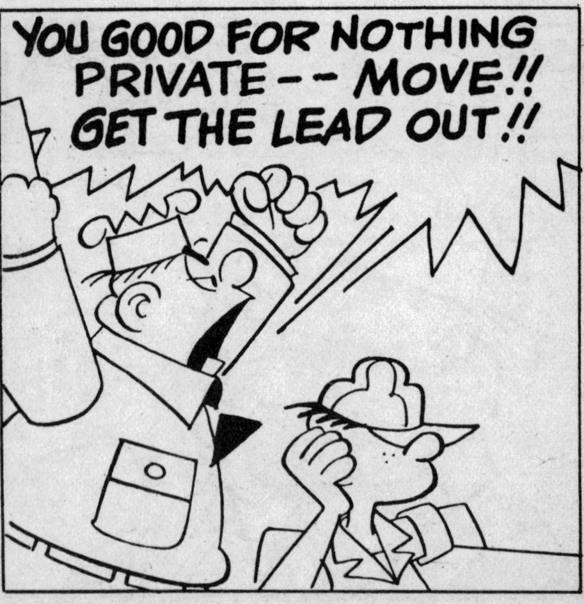
YOU GOOD FOR NOTHING
PRIVATE-- MOVE!!
GET THE LEAD OUT!!

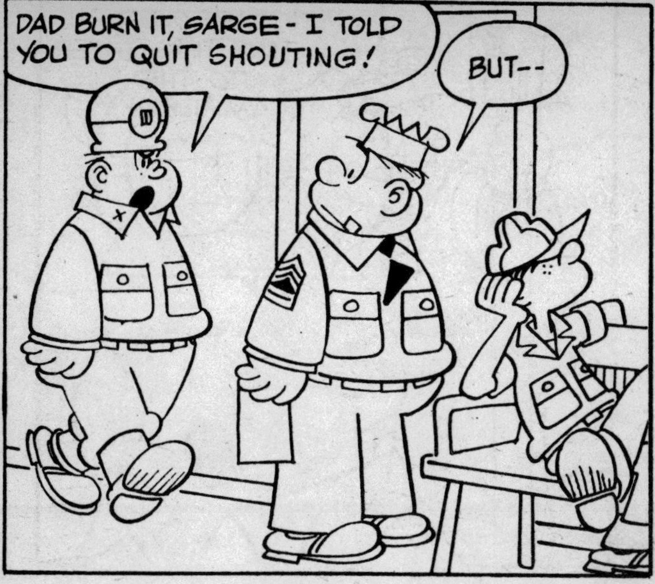
DAD BURN IT, SARGE - I TOLD YOU TO QUIT SHOUTING!
BUT--

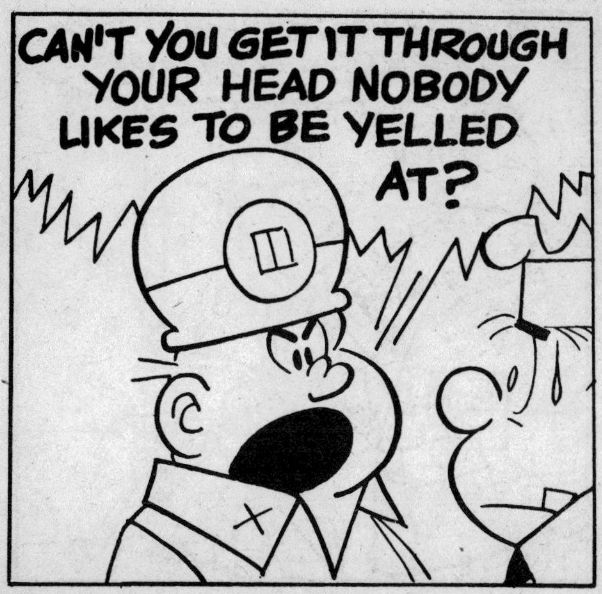
CAN'T YOU GET IT THROUGH YOUR HEAD NOBODY LIKES TO BE YELLED AT?

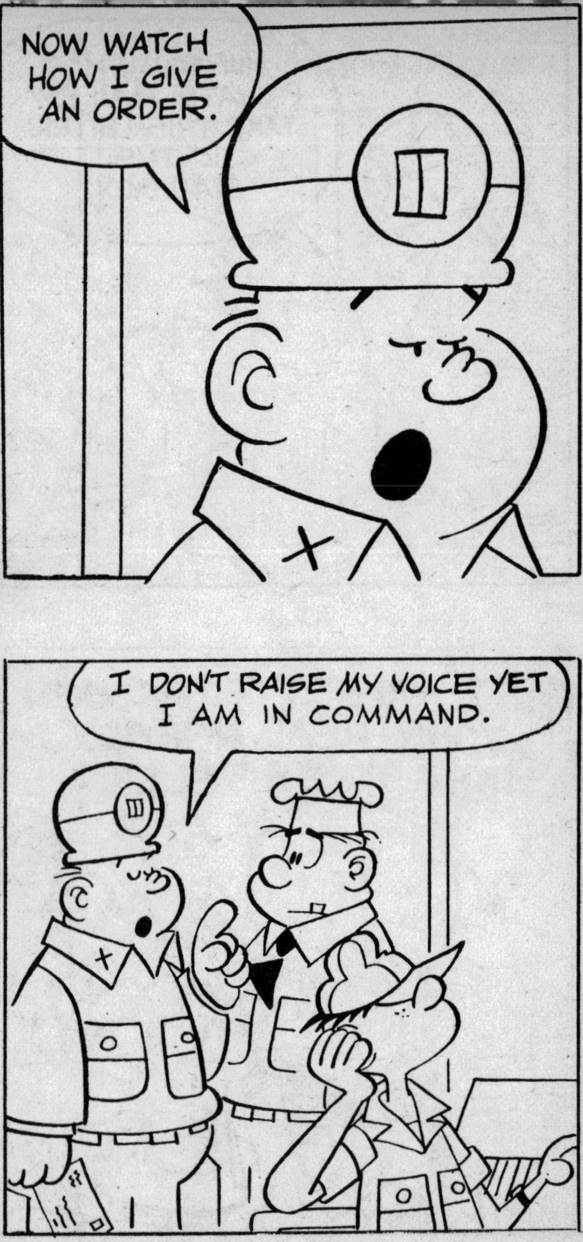
NOW WATCH HOW I GIVE AN ORDER.
I DON'T RAISE MY VOICE YET I AM IN COMMAND.

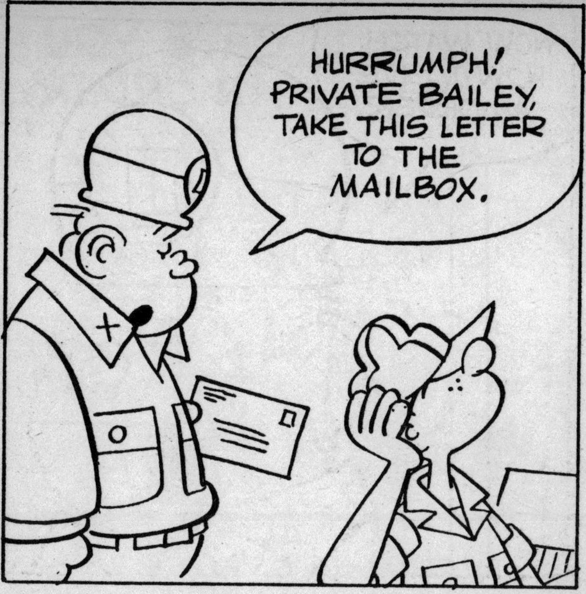
HURRUMPH! PRIVATE BAILEY, TAKE THIS LETTER TO THE MAILBOX.

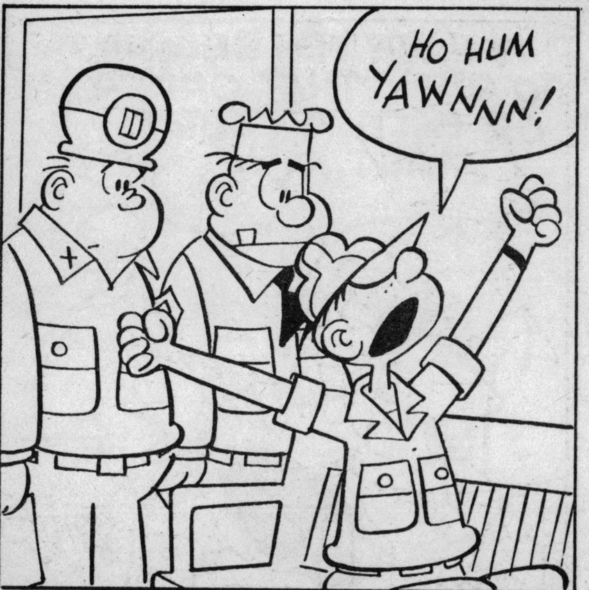
HO HUM YAWNNNN!

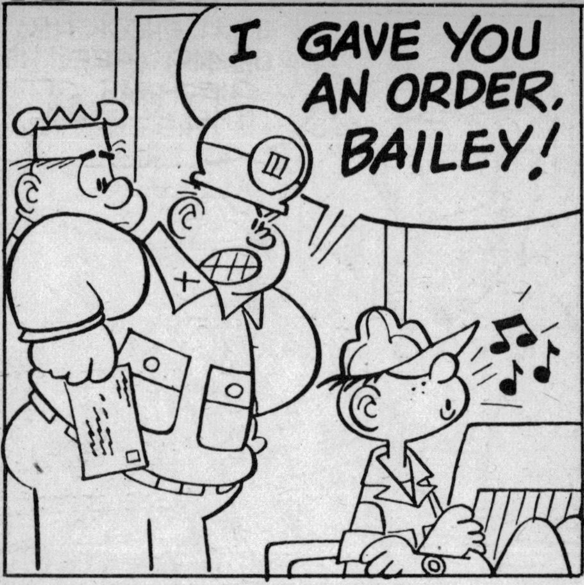
I GAVE YOU AN ORDER, BAILEY!

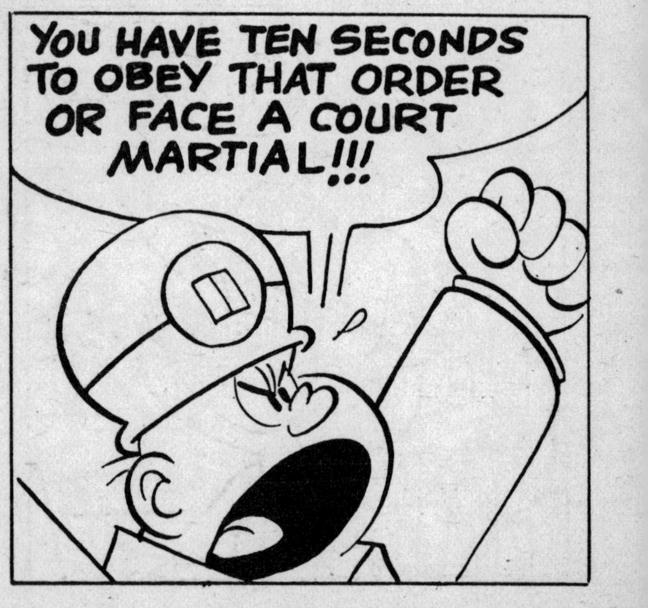
YOU HAVE TEN SECONDS TO OBEY THAT ORDER OR FACE A COURT MARTIAL!!!

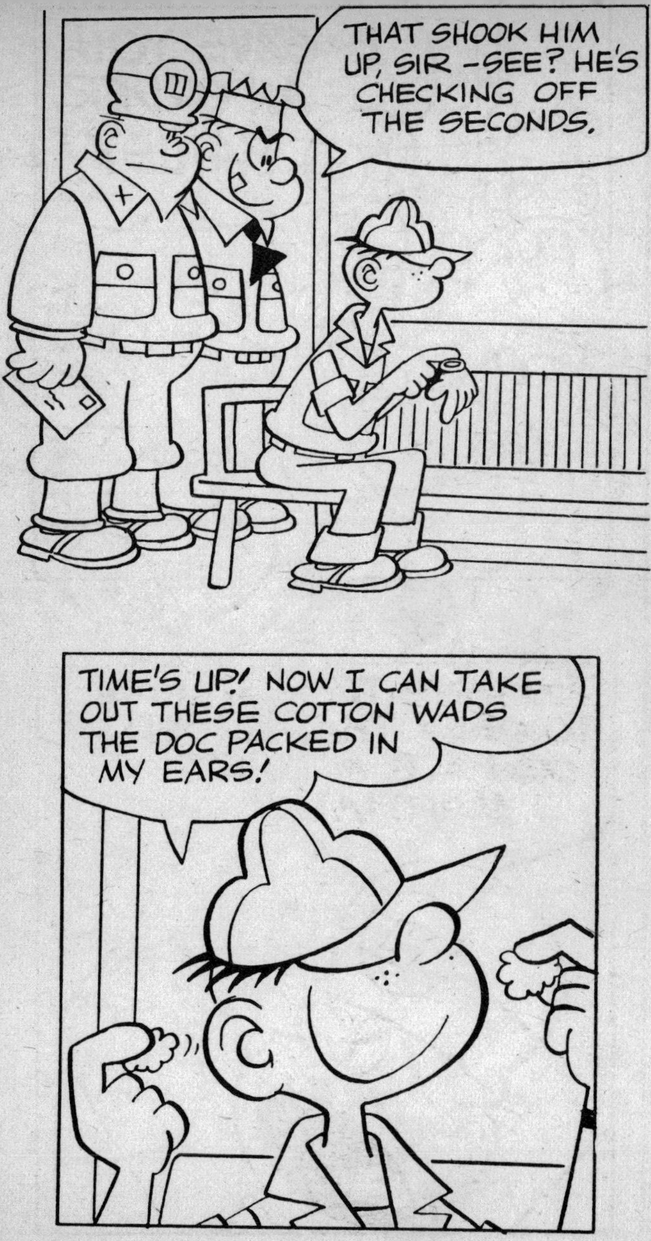
THAT SHOOK HIM UP, SIR –SEE? HE'S CHECKING OFF THE SECONDS.
TIME'S UP! NOW I CAN TAKE OUT THESE COTTON WADS THE DOC PACKED IN MY EARS!

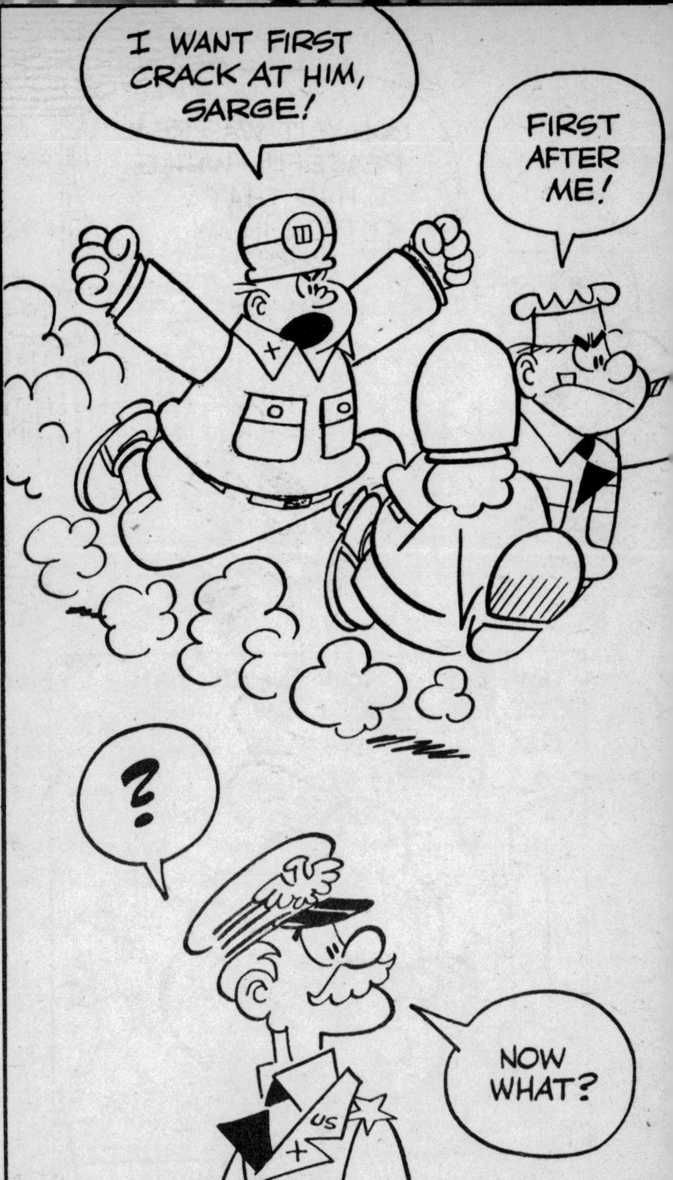
I WANT FIRST CRACK AT HIM, SARGE!
FIRST AFTER ME!
?
NOW WHAT?

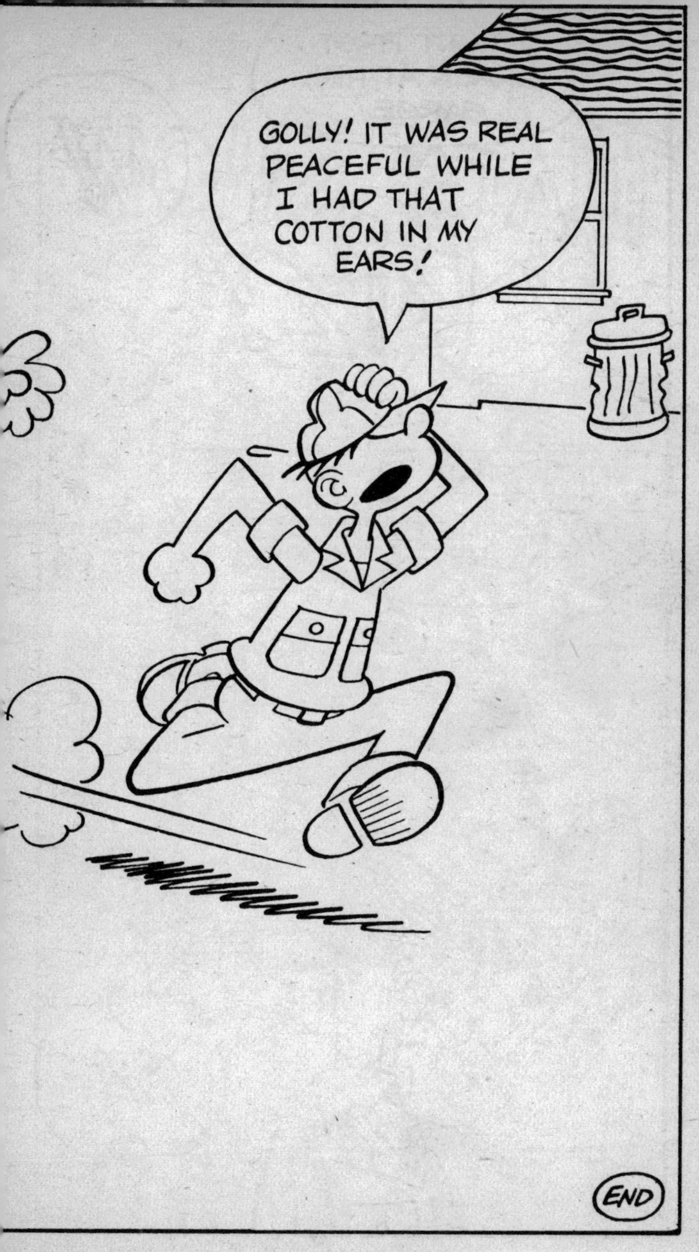
GOLLY! IT WAS REAL PEACEFUL WHILE I HAD THAT COTTON IN MY EARS!
END

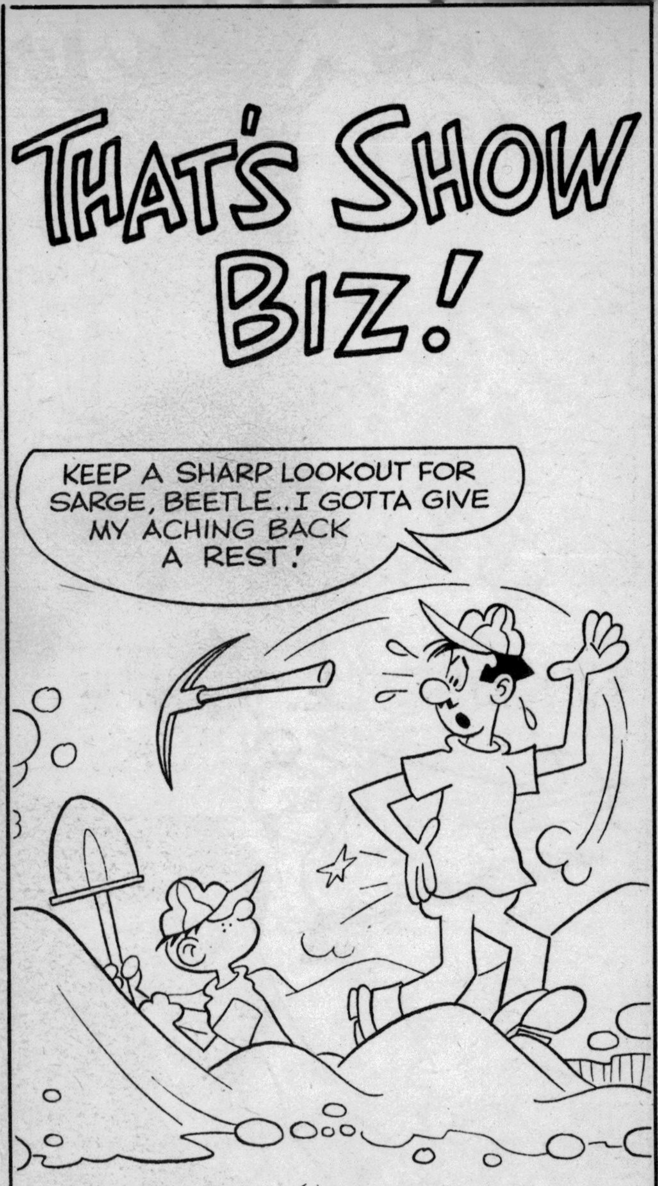
THAT'S SHOW BIZ!
KEEP A SHARP LOOKOUT FOR SARGE, BEETLE..I GOTTA GIVE MY ACHING BACK A REST!

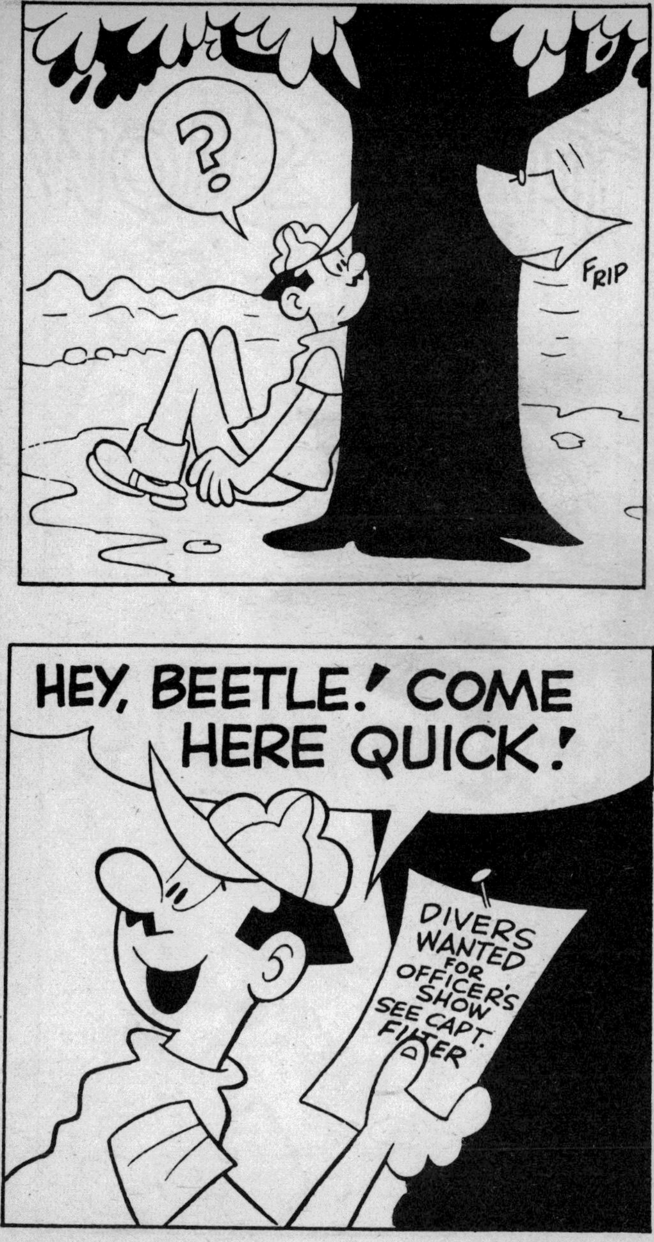
?
FRIP
HEY, BEETLE! COME HERE QUICK!
DIVERS WANTED FOR OFFICER'S SHOW SEE CAPT.

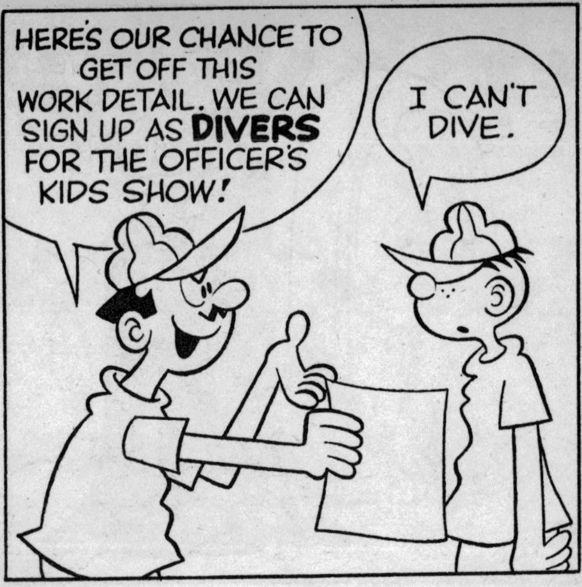
HERE'S OUR CHANCE TO GET OFF THIS WORK DETAIL. WE CAN SIGN UP AS **DIVERS** FOR THE OFFICER'S KIDS SHOW!
I CAN'T DIVE.

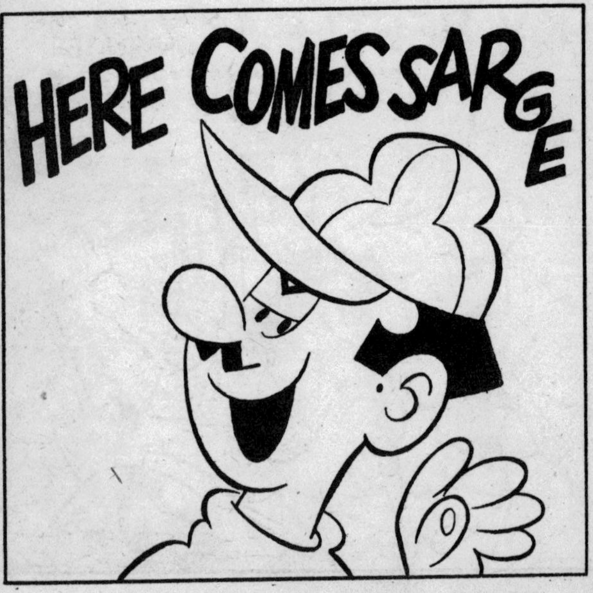
HERE COMES SARGE

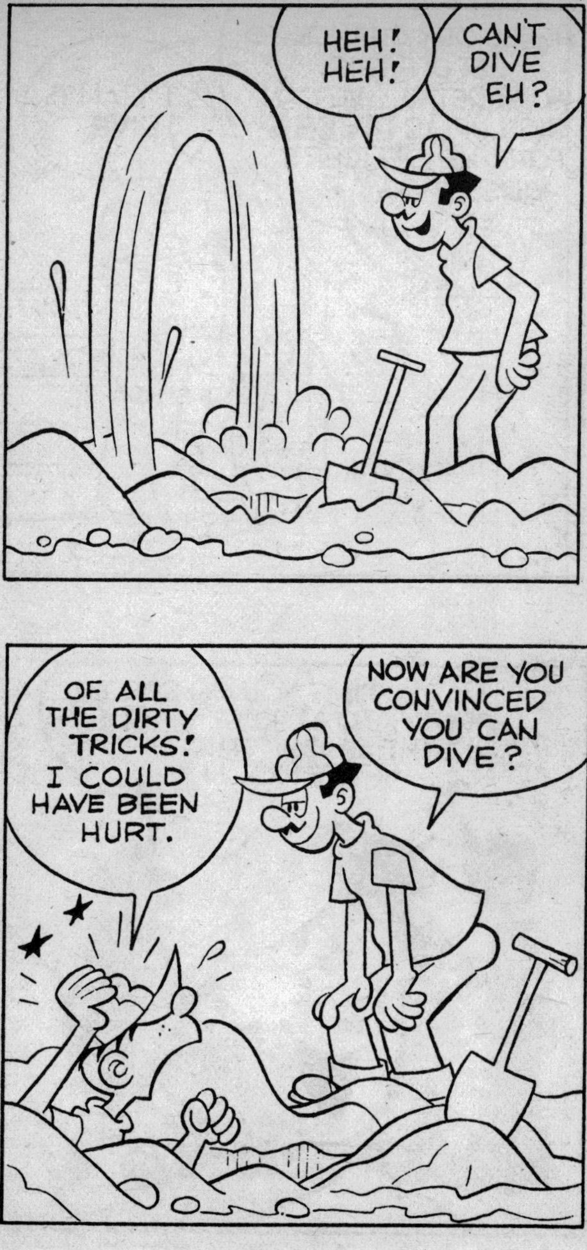
HEH! HEH!
CAN'T DIVE EH?
NOW ARE YOU CONVINCED YOU CAN DIVE?
OF ALL THE DIRTY TRICKS! I COULD HAVE BEEN HURT.

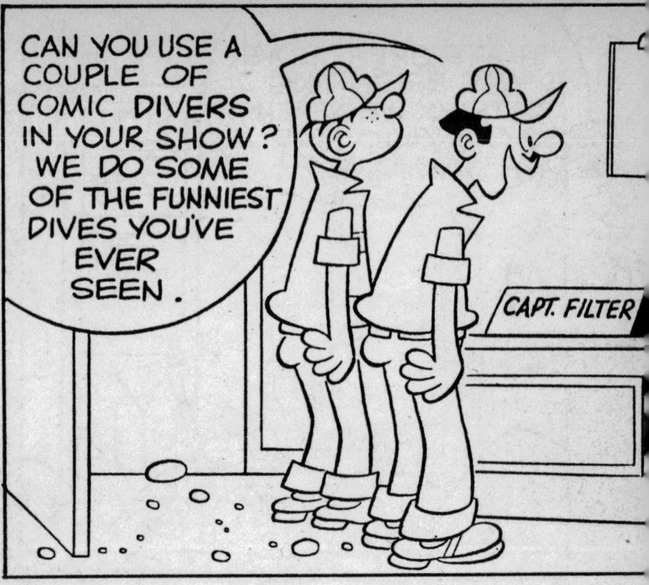
CAN YOU USE A COUPLE OF COMIC DIVERS IN YOUR SHOW? WE DO SOME OF THE FUNNIEST DIVES YOU'VE EVER SEEN.
CAPT. FILTER

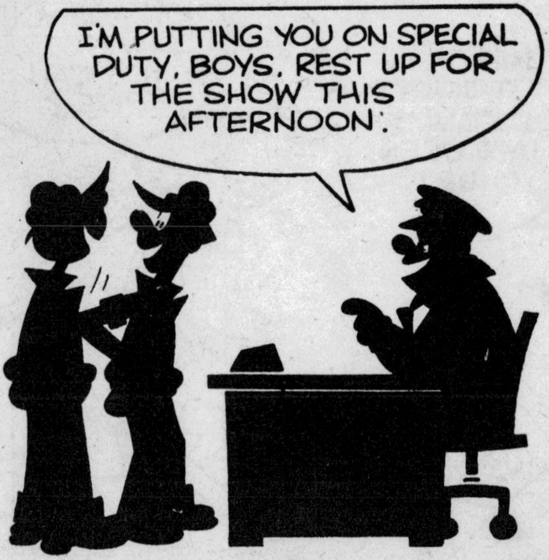
I'M PUTTING YOU ON SPECIAL DUTY, BOYS. REST UP FOR THE SHOW THIS AFTERNOON.

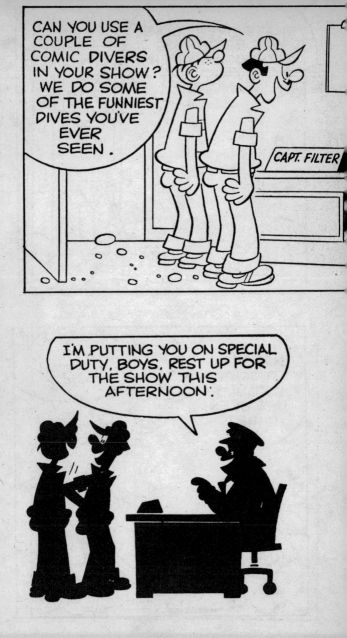

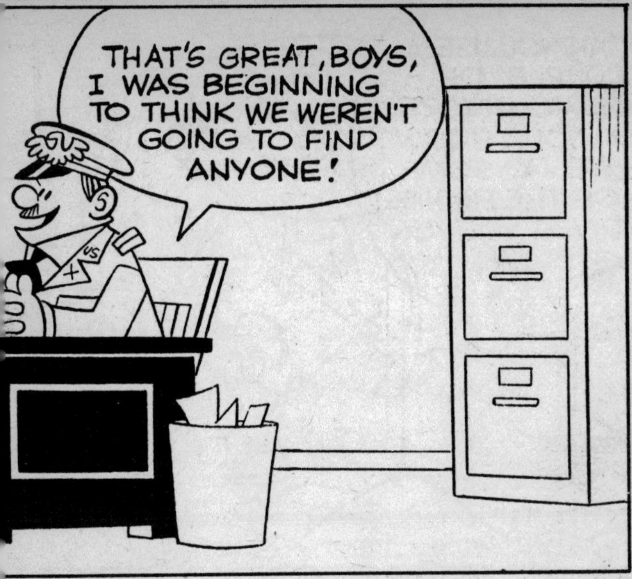
THAT'S GREAT, BOYS, I WAS BEGINNING TO THINK WE WEREN'T GOING TO FIND ANYONE!

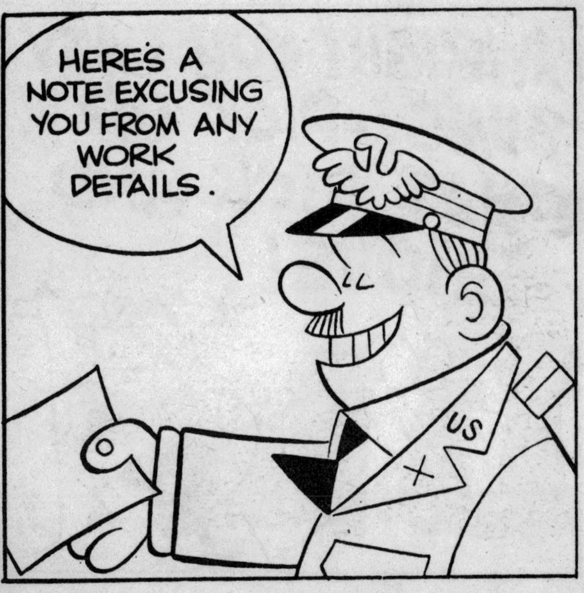
HERE'S A NOTE EXCUSING YOU FROM ANY WORK DETAILS.

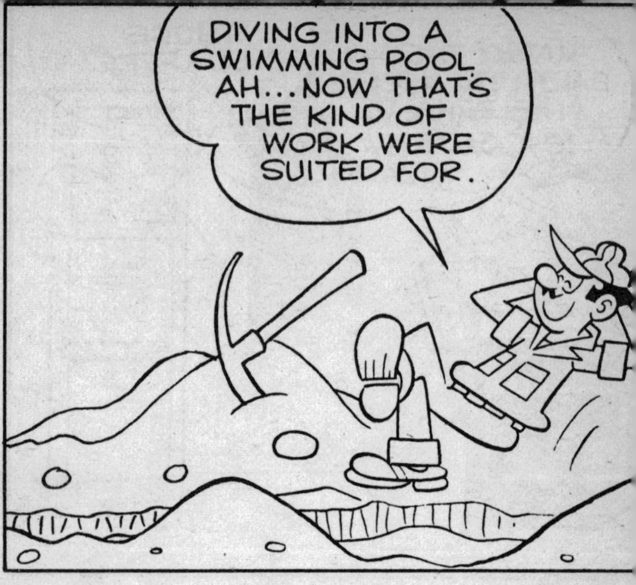

DIVING INTO A SWIMMING POOL. AH...NOW THAT'S THE KIND OF WORK WE'RE SUITED FOR.

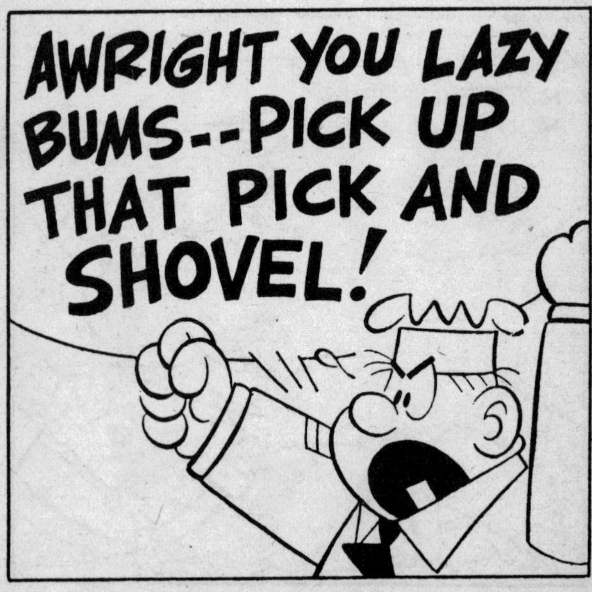

AWRIGHT YOU LAZY BUMS--PICK UP THAT PICK AND SHOVEL!

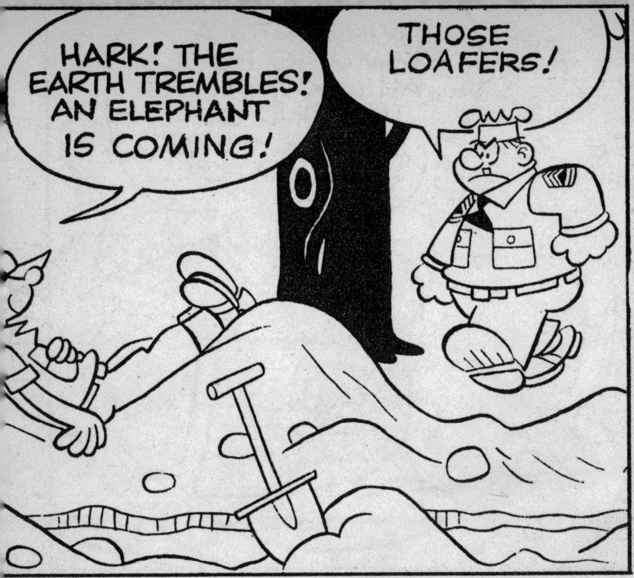
HARK! THE EARTH TREMBLES! AN ELEPHANT IS COMING!
THOSE LOAFERS!

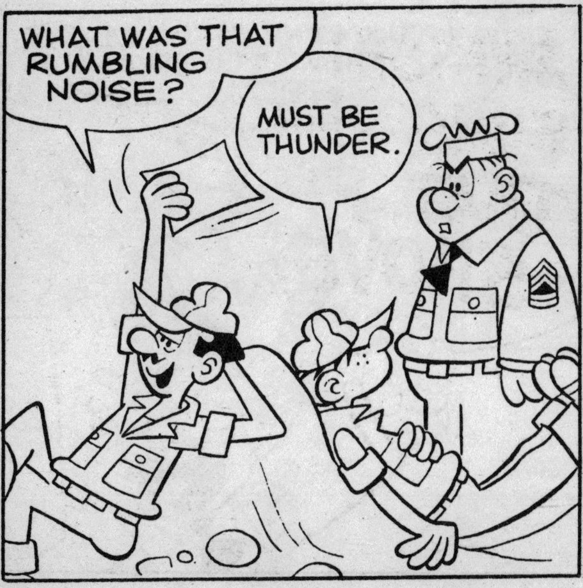
WHAT WAS THAT RUMBLING NOISE?
MUST BE THUNDER.

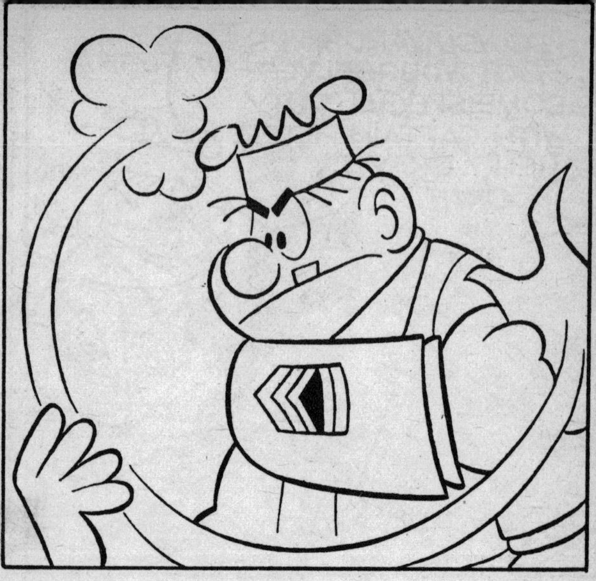

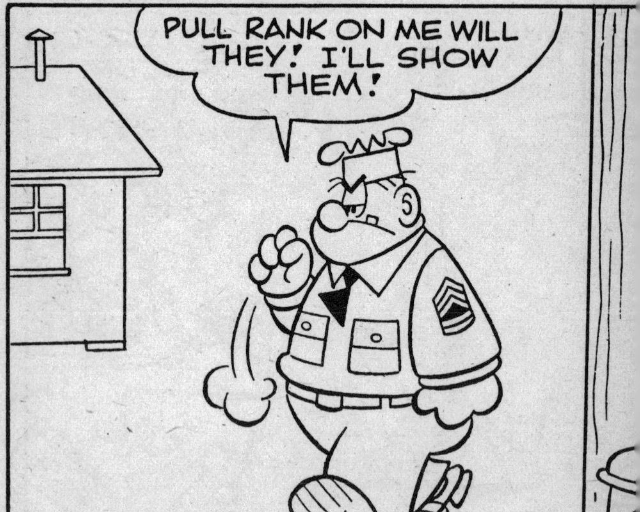
PULL RANK ON ME WILL THEY! I'LL SHOW THEM!

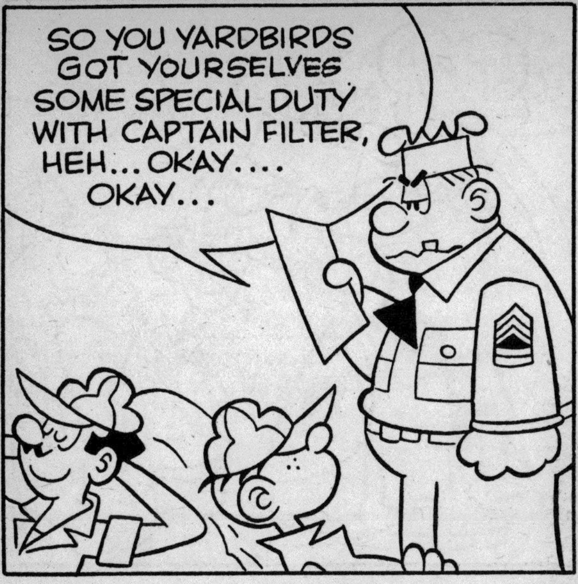
SO YOU YARDBIRDS GOT YOURSELVES SOME SPECIAL DUTY WITH CAPTAIN FILTER, HEH... OKAY.... OKAY...

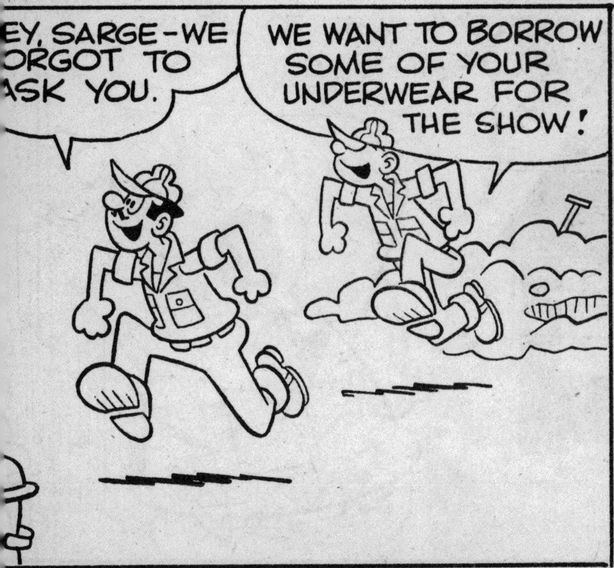
EY, SARGE-WE ORGOT TO ASK YOU.
WE WANT TO BORROW SOME OF YOUR UNDERWEAR FOR THE SHOW!

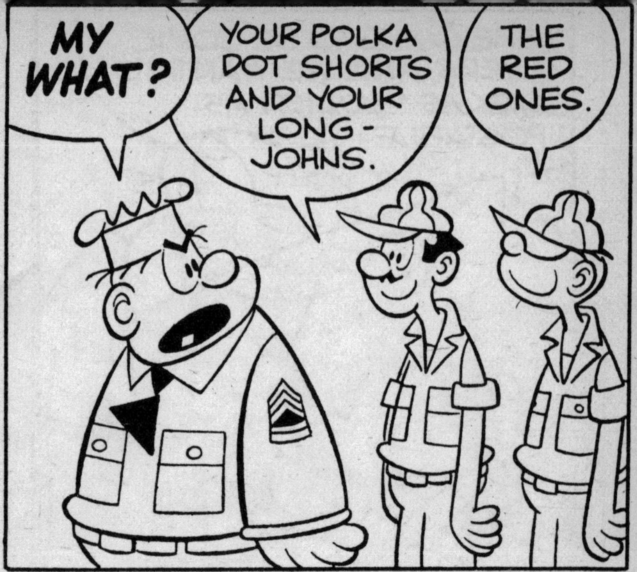
MY WHAT?
YOUR POLKA DOT SHORTS AND YOUR LONG-JOHNS.
THE RED ONES.

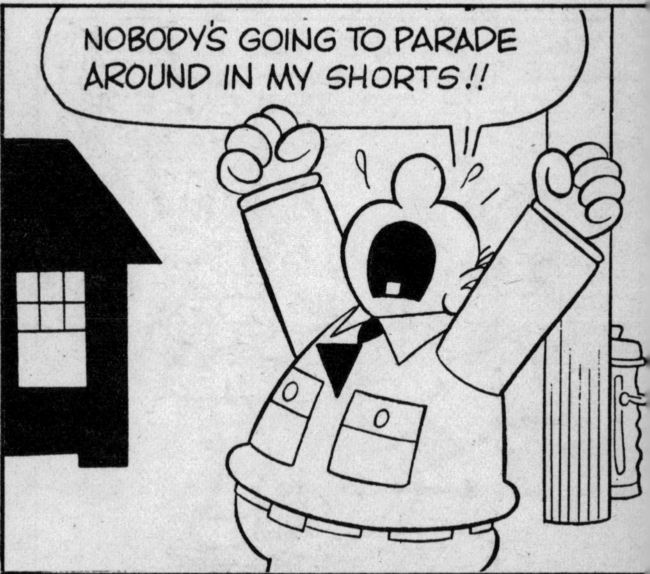
NOBODY'S GOING TO PARADE AROUND IN MY SHORTS!!

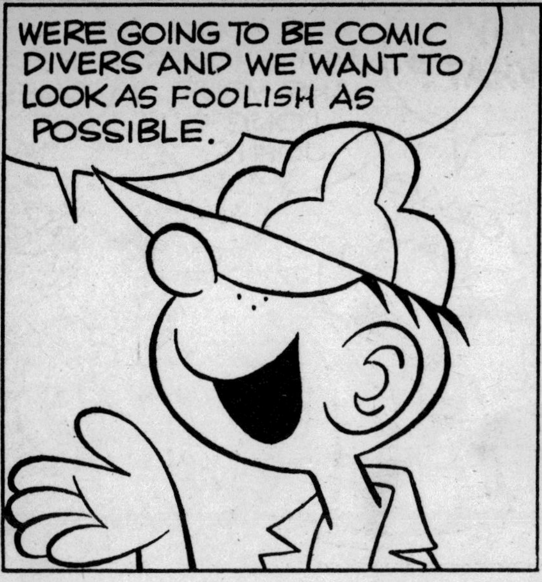
WERE GOING TO BE COMIC DIVERS AND WE WANT TO LOOK AS FOOLISH AS POSSIBLE.

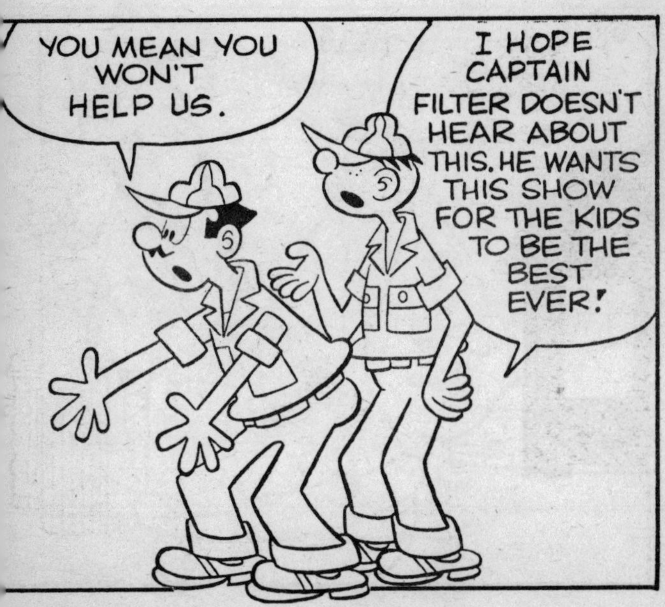
YOU MEAN YOU WON'T HELP US.
I HOPE CAPTAIN FILTER DOESN'T HEAR ABOUT THIS. HE WANTS THIS SHOW FOR THE KIDS TO BE THE BEST EVER!

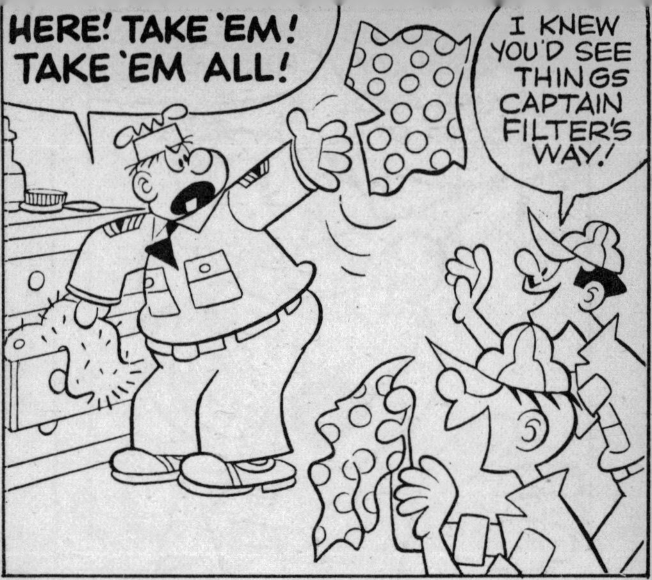
HERE! TAKE 'EM! TAKE 'EM ALL!
I KNEW YOU'D SEE THINGS CAPTAIN FILTER'S WAY!

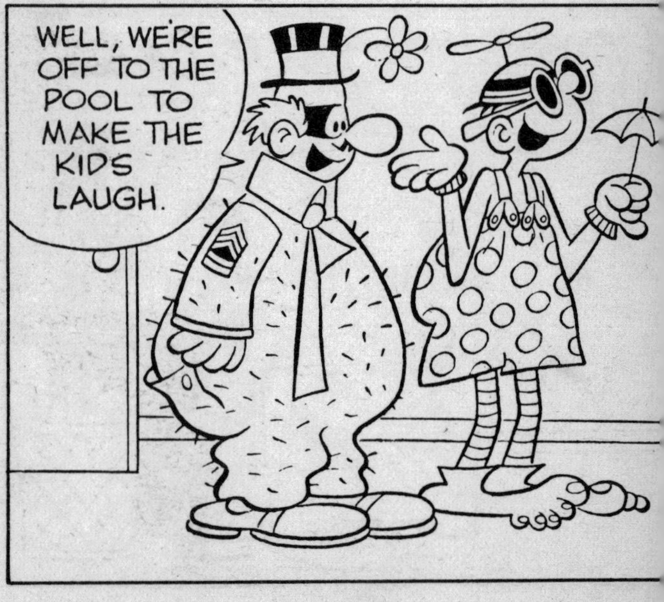
WELL, WE'RE OFF TO THE POOL TO MAKE THE KIDS LAUGH.

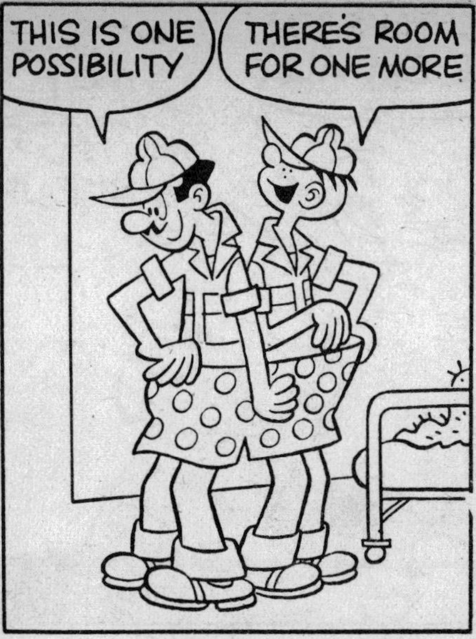
THIS IS ONE POSSIBILITY
THERE'S ROOM FOR ONE MORE

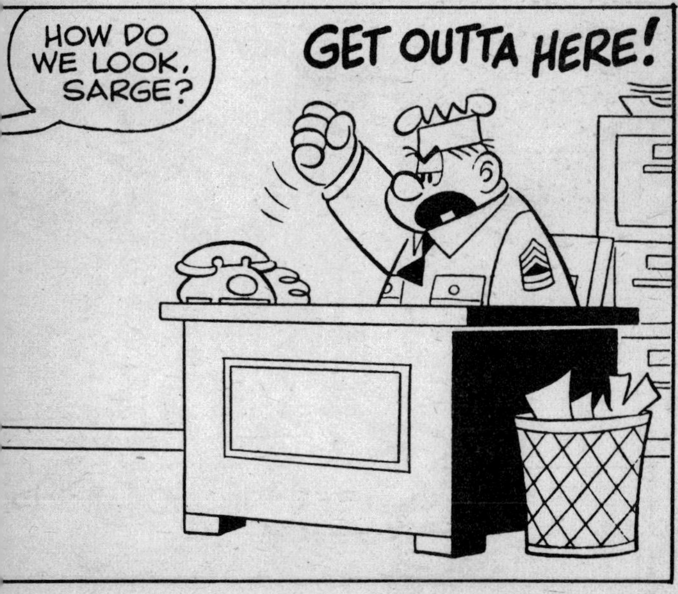
HOW DO WE LOOK, SARGE?
GET OUTTA HERE!

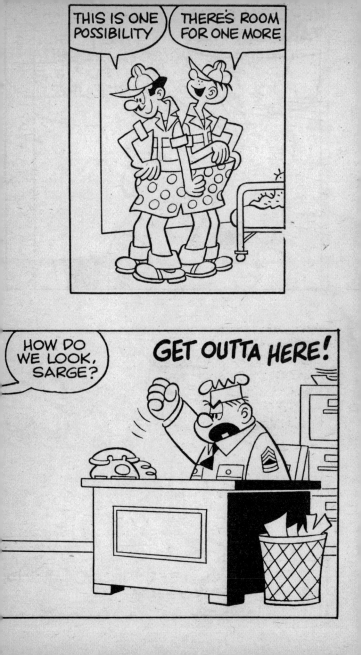

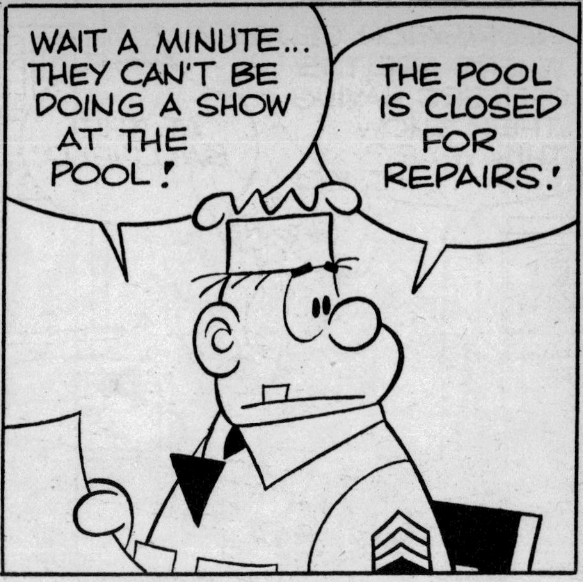
WAIT A MINUTE... THEY CAN'T BE DOING A SHOW AT THE POOL!
THE POOL IS CLOSED FOR REPAIRS!

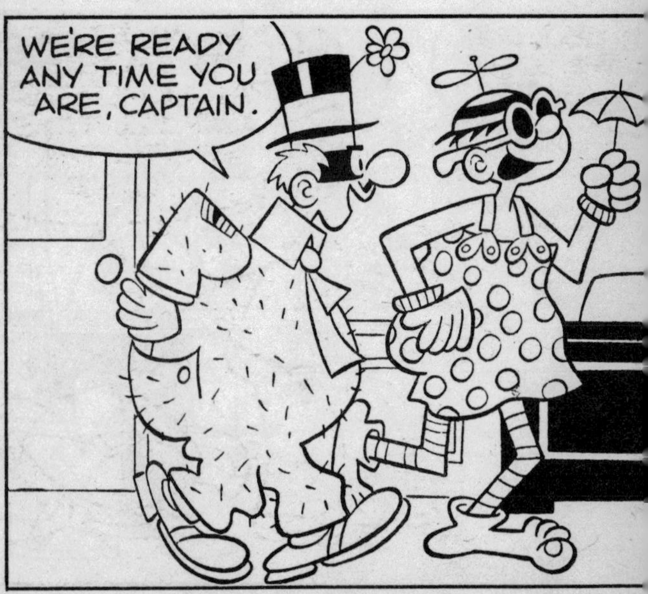
WE'RE READY ANY TIME YOU ARE, CAPTAIN.

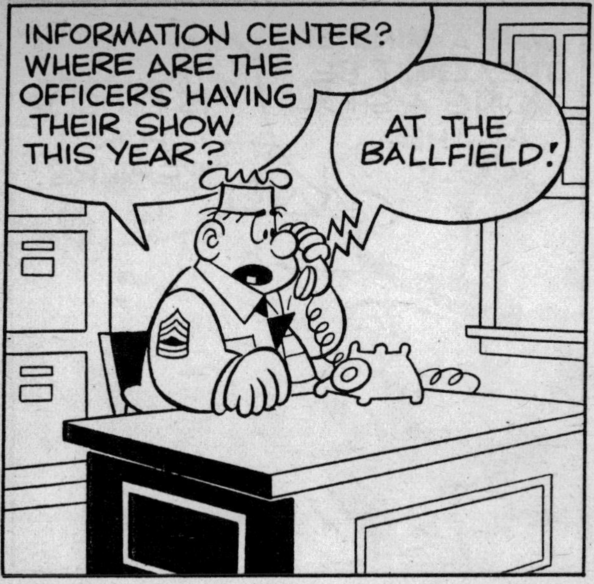
INFORMATION CENTER? WHERE ARE THE OFFICERS HAVING THEIR SHOW THIS YEAR?
AT THE BALLFIELD!

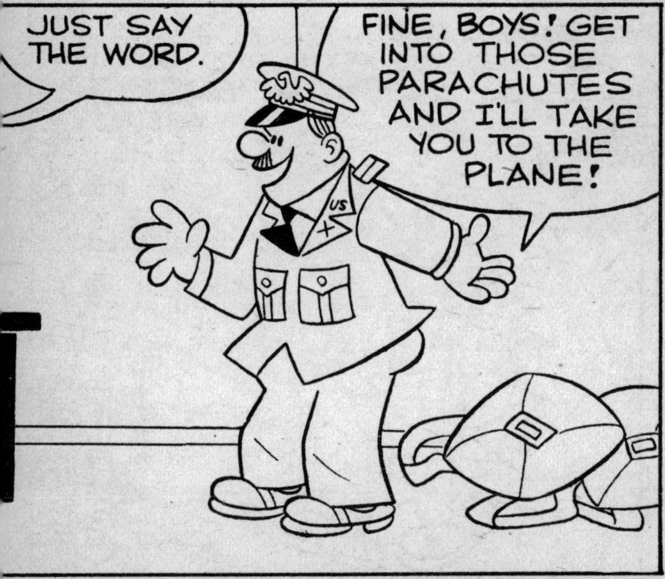
JUST SAY THE WORD.
FINE, BOYS! GET INTO THOSE PARACHUTES AND I'LL TAKE YOU TO THE PLANE!
US

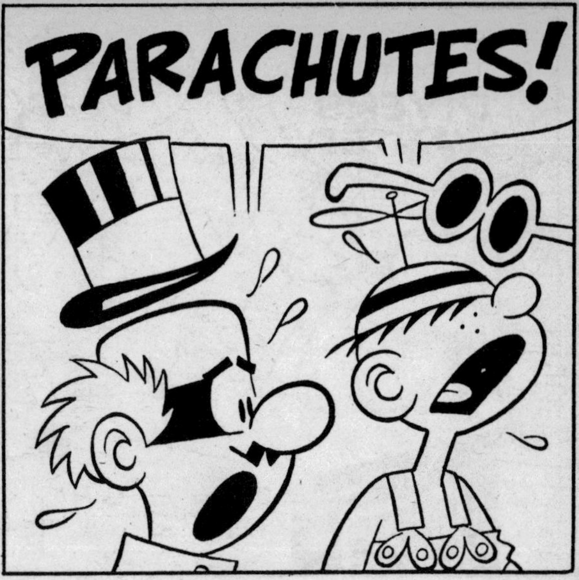
PARACHUTES!

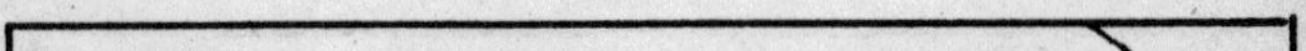
YOU MADE A MISTAKE ON THIS NOTICE, OTIS, IT'S SUPPOSED TO SAY SKY-DIVERS WANTED.
US

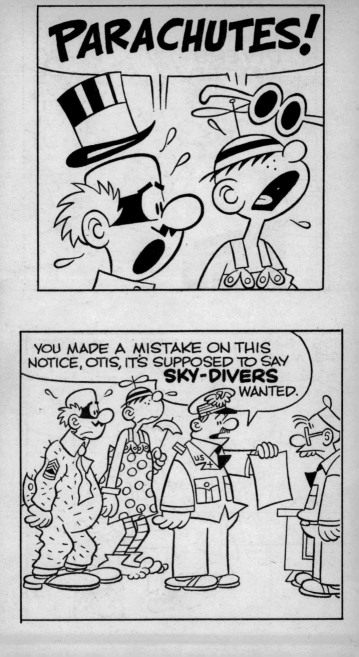

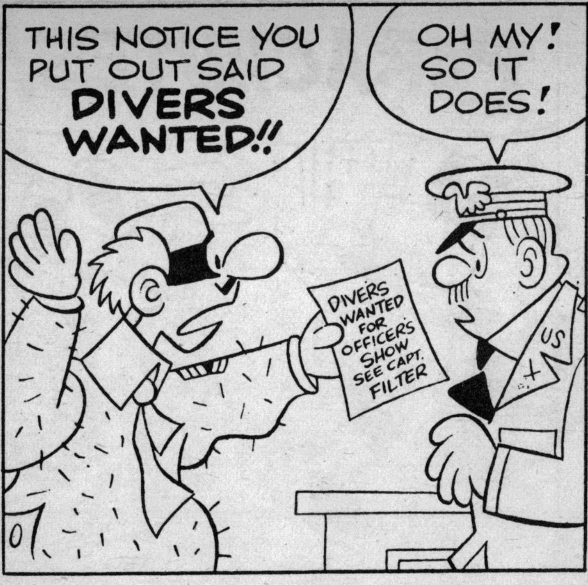
THIS NOTICE YOU PUT OUT SAID DIVERS WANTED!!
OH MY! SO IT DOES!
DIVERS WANTED FOR OFFICER'S SHOW SEE CAPT. FILTER

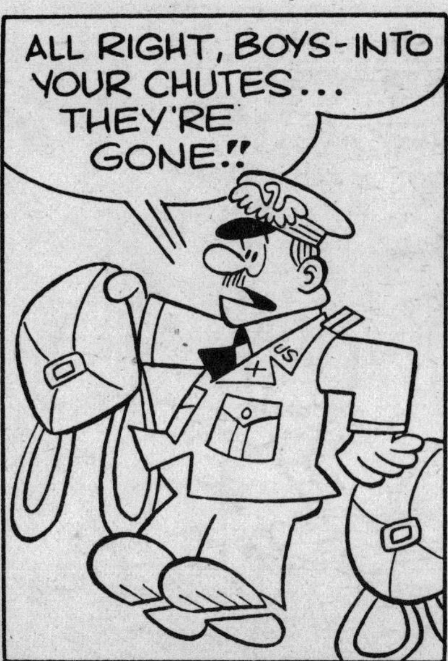
ALL RIGHT, BOYS-INTO YOUR CHUTES... THEY'RE GONE!!

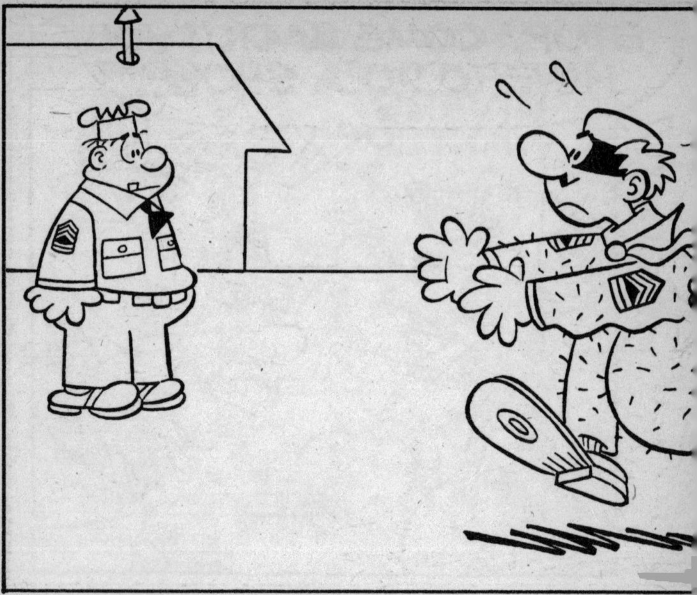

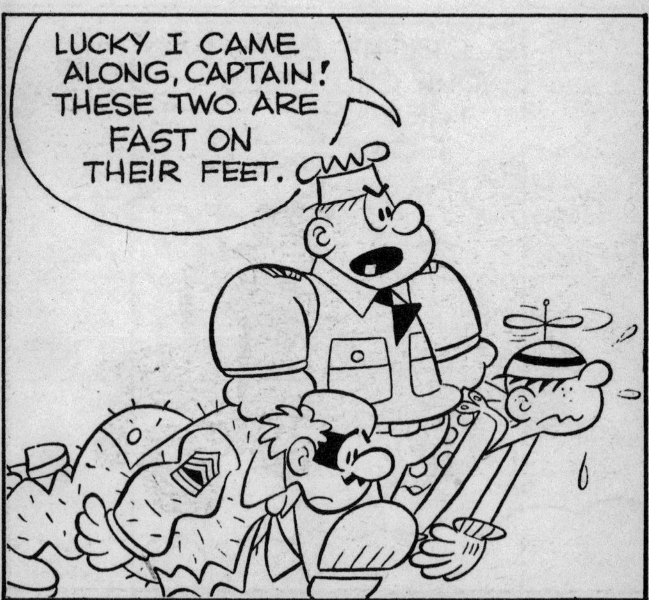
LUCKY I CAME ALONG, CAPTAIN! THESE TWO ARE FAST ON THEIR FEET.

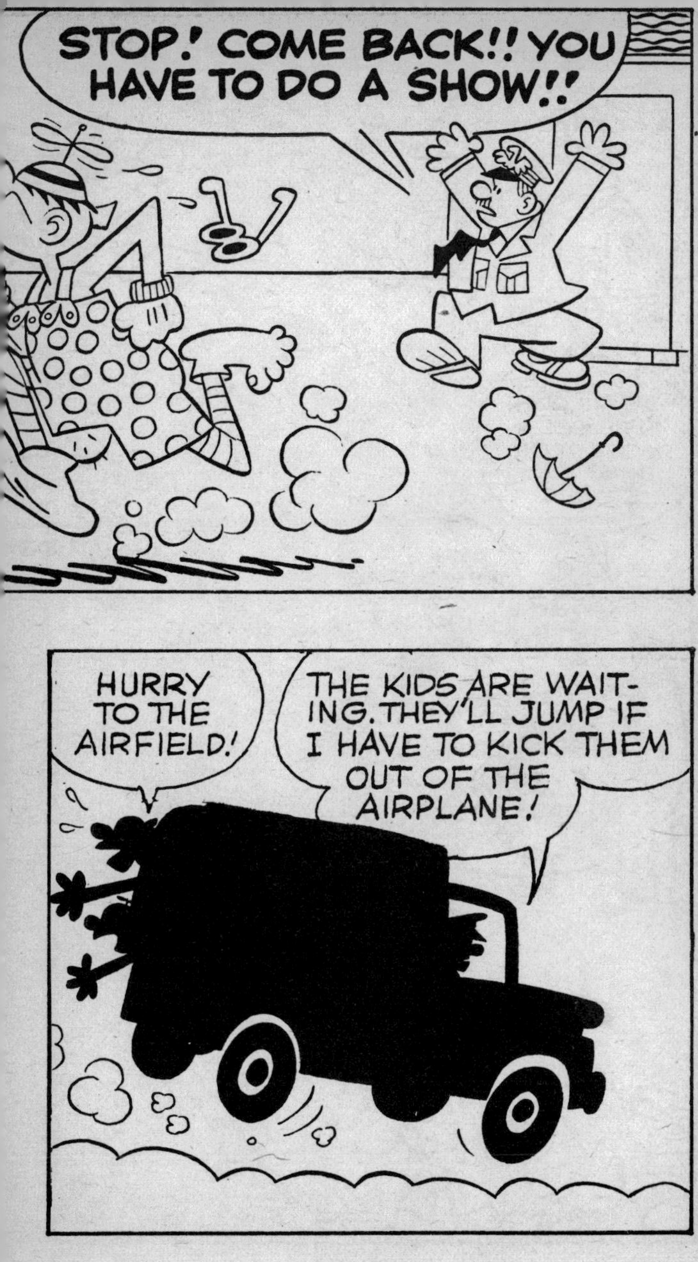
STOP! COME BACK!! YOU HAVE TO DO A SHOW!!
HURRY TO THE AIRFIELD!
THE KIDS ARE WAIT-ING. THEY'LL JUMP IF I HAVE TO KICK THEM OUT OF THE AIRPLANE!

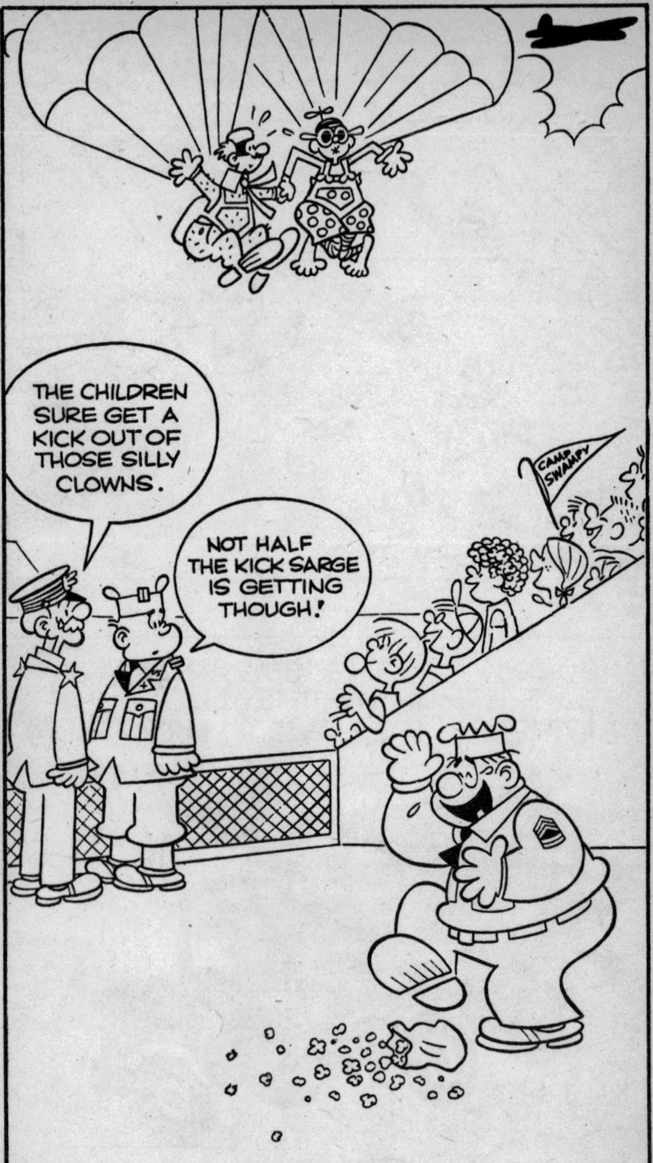
THE CHILDREN SURE GET A KICK OUT OF THOSE SILLY CLOWNS.
NOT HALF THE KICK SARGE IS GETTING THOUGH!
CAMP SWAMPY
The END